LUCKY JOHN

LUCKY JOHN

FROM TEA BOY TO CHAIRMAN
OF A MULTI-BILLION POUND FIRM

JOHN BROWN

with David Ashforth

DEDICATION

I dedicate this book to my father John Lawrence Brown (Sapper 2144361 Royal Engineers), a brave, kind and good man. Devoted husband to my mother Iris. He firmly believed it was the duty of every parent to try to ensure that their children had a better start in life than they had had. His interest in and passion for racing ignited a flame in me that has burned bright ever since. I owe every bit of my success to the start he gave me.

Published in 2004 by Highdown,
an imprint of Raceform Ltd
Compton, Newbury, Berkshire, RG20 6NL
Raceform Ltd is a wholly-owned subsidiary of Trinity Mirror plc

A catalogue record for this book is available from the British Library.

ISBN 1-904317-30-8

Designed by Tracey Scarlett
Printed by CPD, Wales

CONTENTS

FOREWORD

Regrets, yes there will always be a few. But for me, to misquote Mr Sinatra, there is one that must be mentioned. I wish that I had worked with John Brown. It would have been, let's use the words carefully, a challenging, sometimes exasperating, but overall life enhancing experience. This book will tell you why.

For John is much, much more than the driven East Ender who started with William Hills as a teenager and then worked all the hours god gave to Cain to graft his way upward and then survive the boardroom traumas of the Brent Walker drama to end as the most successful bookmaker ever to walk away from power. He is very direct but there is wisdom to match the work ethic. And, as you might guess, it doesn't owe much to modern management speak.

"I'm hard," he says in one memorable passage, "but my leadership style isn't autocratic. Autocracy is when you impose your will without listening to anybody. You have to listen, and the arguments have to be hammered out over the table then, and only then are you in a position to make a decision."

He doesn't believe in consensus – "you never take the best decision, you always accept less than the best" – and absolutely doesn't "do" appraisals. "It's a waste of time. If a tiger's got stripes, its no use sending him to the cleaners to have his stripes washed off." Yet he does believe in people: "I see people's strengths and ignore their weaknesses," and above all he understands, and indeed loves the business of betting and horseracing.

That is what is ultimately so attractive about the man. He comes from a tough background so why should contact be anything less than direct - "diplomacy is often about fudging an issue"- but at heart he adores the game, the people, the puzzles, and above all the horses at the centre of it all. No leading figure in the whole racing activity takes as keen an interest in the minutiae of form and speed figures - as our computer programmers tend to find out when the great man's laptop turns up a glitch in our system.

Racing and betting have been lucky to have thrown up some remarkable figures down the years. Read this and see how John Brown came to be amongst them.

Brough Scott
London, 2004

CHAPTER ONE
GET THE BATH OFF THE WALL

It was a happy childhood. When I was two years old, a bomb went off nearby and I went flying across the living room and crashed through the glass door into our shop. It wasn't something you wanted to do too often, because glass doors were a rarity in Chobham Road. After that, my mum took me off to Slough for a while. John Betjeman was all for bombs being dropped on Slough – "Come, friendly bombs, and fall on Slough. It isn't fit for humans now." Luckily for me, the bombs didn't drop on the bit of Slough to which we had been sent.

By the end of the Second World War, Chobham Road was still there, halfway between Stratford and Leyton, in London's East End, but the area was a bit short on houses. Our shop was one of the few buildings still standing.

People sometimes say that I sound like an East End barrow boy but we didn't have a barrow and didn't sell vegetables. My grandmother had bought a newsagent's shop in Chobham Road for about £50 during the war so that, when my dad got back from serving in the army, he wouldn't have to go back to working on the railways. Fifty pounds was cheap, unless the shop got hit by a bomb, in which case it was expensive, because there was no insurance against bomb damage.

My father, who was also called John, was a good man. I couldn't have wished for a better father or teacher about life. He was the best sort of father anyone could ever hope to have, and a brave man, too. When the war broke out he could have carried on working on the railway but he volunteered to work at the Woolwich Arsenal and then joined the Royal Engineers and served in North Africa and Italy.

He was away when I was born, on 17 September 1942, and when he came back he would never talk about the war. When I asked him what he'd got his Oak Leaf medal for, which meant that he'd been recommended for a gallantry award, he always said it was for having been the first into the NAAFI queue three times in a row.

Ours was a strange old house, big and shambling, with an attic and a large cellar. My great grandad and great grandmum lived in the attic while the gas cooker and tin bath lived in the cellar, which only had one small, skylight window. There was no running hot water, only one fire, in the room behind the shop, and an outside toilet. My dad built a wooden 'lean-to' over the toilet, to convert it into a semi-indoor toilet. For Chobham Road, that was quite posh. Later, he installed a small Ascot gas water-heater over the sink in the basement. The heater didn't have a flue. Instead, we had a sheet of asbestos on the ceiling to absorb the heat. I don't know where the carbon monoxide fumes went but the house was so draughty that I expect they just swopped places with the draughts.

In the winter, it was so cold that ice used to form on the inside of the bedroom window panes. Once a week, we'd take the bath off the wall and all wash in the same water, one after the other. There was my mum and dad, my gran and grandad, and my great gran and great grandad. The hot water came from a copper container, heated from underneath by a coal fire, which took several hours to heat up. We'd use a saucepan to ladle the water out of it, into the bath. The copper just provided enough hot water for one bath full. On other days, they'd stand me in a bowl of water on the kitchen table, and wash me in that. Later, like my dad, I'd wash in the kitchen sink. You'd come down fully dressed, take your shirt off, wash your face and armpits, put your shirt back on and go to work. There were no deodorants. Everyone smoked, and we must all have stunk to high heaven, although no one seemed to notice. I suppose everyone was the same.

As a small child, my mum, Iris, had been taken in and cared for by an aunt, who we knew as nan. My mum's own mother had died and her father abandoned her. Mum worked at Yardley's perfume factory in Stratford. I think the building's still there. To me, it looks like a big toilet, covered in tiles, but in those days it was an architectural revelation for the East End.

Mum met my dad at a youth club and was always completely devoted to him. After the war, they never spent a day out of each other's company until the day he died. She was just there, doing what he wanted, and seemed very happy. It was different in those days. She's still alive today; a lovely lady, my mum. Dad and my gran ran the shop. People talk about Asian corner shops opening all hours but it's nothing new. Our shop was open from 6.00am to 10.30pm every day except Sunday, when it shut at 7.00pm.

I grew up in the shop. It was a newsagent's and tobacconist's and all the customers were poor people. They'd come in and ask for one razor blade or one cigarette. We had to split up the packets so they could afford to buy them. I went to Colgrave Road Primary School in Stratford. It was very run down but the teachers were fantastic. We'd get to school early to play football in the playground and, once a week, we went to the council pitch at Temple Mills. The 'skins' versus the 'vests'. Those who had a vest played for the vests, and those who didn't played for the skins. Apart from the two goalkeepers, the other 20 or more of us all chased the ball wildly around the pitch. Mr Duffy, the teacher, tried to explain that we didn't all have to chase it at the same time but we did. Maybe it was because there was no television to copy from in those days. Mr Duffy must have been so dedicated, working in a run-down school in a poor area, yet always giving up his own time for us.

The pitch was made from cinders, and you didn't see any sliding tackles on that. I used to play for the school team. The school colours were red shirts with black sleeves but the shirts were so old and had been washed so many times that they were actually pink with grey sleeves.

Later, when I was at Stratford Grammar School, I was picked to play for their team and dad let me off my Saturday job, which was collecting the money from the people to whom I'd delivered newspapers during the week. I scored, for the one and only time, and was never picked again. I wasn't really brave or tough enough for football. I was better at cricket; I loved that. The primary-school team boasted two bats and two pads and one set of stumps and I used to open the batting, on the cinder pitch, which was covered with a coconut mat.

Outside school, kids would play in the streets or on bomb sites and parents didn't seem to worry about their safety. There seemed no need to worry. There were no televisions – certainly not in Chobham Road. There was virtually no traffic and the milkman and greengrocer both made their deliveries with a horse-drawn cart. Usually, we played either football or cricket but sometimes we'd play our version of ice hockey, using wooden sticks with extra bits nailed on the ends, and a flattened tin can as the puck. Other times we'd knock the spokes out of a bicycle wheel and have a race, driving the wheel along by hitting it with a stick. That was on our speedway track, which we built on a bomb site, with discarded house bricks marking out the track.

Kids of all ages took part in these street games, which were organised by the older children, without any adult involvement. No favours were asked, and none were given, but I don't remember there ever being any trouble, just lots of fun. Looking back, I think they were very character-building. The games were highly competitive, with everyone given their chance, regardless of age. As a five-year-old, I remember playing cricket and facing up to a 14-year-old bowler, bowling flat out. At that age, you lasted until he bowled a straight ball, and hit the wicket, which was a wooden board with the stumps drawn on it in chalk. If the ball hit the board, and there was chalk on the ball, you were out. The street games taught you how to interact with other people and how to look after yourself. They also instilled a competitive spirit in you, a desire to win and a toughness that stood me and others of my generation in good stead throughout our lives.

At school, the only subject in which I was ever interested was mathematics. I could bury myself in that but not in languages. I couldn't do languages to save my life and couldn't cope with French at all. Luckily, the teachers were pragmatic. At grammar school, my French teacher said: "Brown, you've got no chance of passing a French exam; none whatsoever. I'll tell you what. I won't make a nuisance of myself to you if you don't make a nuisance of yourself to me." That was fine by me, and him, and ended my career in languages. That probably included English, as well.

By 1950, the family consisted of my gran, mum, dad, and my three-year-old sister Iris. I had been given the attic as my bedroom, which was three floors above the only fire in the house. At about that time, when I was eight, dad bought an old, 1933 Wolseley Hornet car. It was the first car in the street, complete with leather seats, a temperature gauge on the end of the bonnet, and a cracked windscreen. It had become cracked while a windscreen wiper was being added as a luxury extra. The car meant freedom. Most summer Sundays, rain or shine, we'd leave the shop at 8.00am, pay the lady next door to look after the shop, and drive through the Blackwall Tunnel to Dymchurch, by the sea, which was a four-hour drive each way but led to a fabulous beach. Southend wasn't good enough for my dad.

The very first holiday I or my sister had was when I was nine and my gran took us both to Butlins at Skegness for a fortnight. I thought it was fantastic, roaming the camp all day, playing on the rowing boats, practising cricket in the nets, with organised events just like Hi-de-Hi! on television. That programme brought back great memories for me. Every night my gran would go to the bathhouse and have a proper bath, with running hot water. As a child, I didn't understand the appeal but I do now. It wasn't until I was 18, in 1960, that we lived in a house with a proper bathroom and no tin bath.

They were great times and we were always happy. I wouldn't change any of it, even if I could. Then, when I was 14, I became ill. My mum thought I was trying to bunk off school but she eventually called the doctor. He thought I might have polio and sent me to Ilford Isolation Hospital. After a few days they decided I didn't have polio after all. I had rheumatic fever, instead, which could lead to heart problems.

The doctor stuck me on a hard wooden board with a wafer-thin mattress on it, lay me on my back and told me that, if I ever wanted to have a proper life, I mustn't move except to go to the toilet. The theory was that my heart mustn't do any work. The treatment was aspirin. Every six hours they gave me six aspirins, which sent me to sleep, then they woke me up to give me six more to send me back to sleep again. The nurses even had to feed me. Visitors were allowed for one hour each day, at 2.00pm. My dad visited me every single day for 12 weeks. As I was in isolation, they wouldn't let him in the room, so he stood outside the window, often in the bitter cold, and talked to me through the window. After 10 weeks I was allowed to sit up and two weeks later I was allowed out. Two years later, just before my GCE exams, the illness recurred and I was back in for the same treatment for another six weeks. Thankfully, I've never had a problem with my health since.

When I got back to school, I'd missed my exams. The headmaster wanted me to stay on to take them the following year but I told him that I wanted to work for William Hill. I was 16, coming up to 17. He was horrified. "You can't go and work for a bookmaker," he said. "What a waste of your life."

*

My mum's brother was a bookmaker called Fred Cooper. Although she didn't have any contact with him, didn't like racing and didn't bet, my dad did, thank God. There were no betting shops then. The only legal betting was on credit, by telephone or post, and cash bets by post, which had to be sent to Scotland. My dad used to post his bets to William Hill, Littlewoods and McLaughlins. There was also illegal street betting. That was rife. Every area had its bookie's runner who collected bets and put them in a series of clock bags, which were closed at various times throughout the afternoon to coincide with the 'off' times of different races.

My dad used to have systems; lots of them. One of them was that he'd back the favourite in the last race at a dog track if the favourite in the last race at that track hadn't won for eight meetings, starting with ten shillings and doubling up until one of these favourites won, although he'd stop after four losers. There seems no logic to it: if the last eight favourites have lost, the next one's no more likely to win than if the last eight favourites have all won. But that's what he did. I guess some punters still do.

My dad's reasoning was that, after a string of losing last-race favourites, the track manager would grade the last race to try and produce a winning favourite to send the customers home happy. He may have been right because in the long run he didn't seem to lose on that system. On Grand National day, he would pick a horse in the big race plus a horse in each of three other races, have a single bet on each of them, any-to-come going on to the other three in half-crown doubles and trebles. He had it off the year E.S.B. won the National at 100-7, in 1956, with all four of his horses winning. He spent days trying to work out how much he'd won – in fact the postal order arrived before he had worked it out. I remember he took me to the local bike shop and bought me a brand new Raleigh, with a double 'clanger', with his winnings. Then he had four winners again the next year, when Sundew won the National at 20-1.

During the war, my dad had become mates with a carpenter from Scotland. He used to spend Christmas with us and he sometimes got tips from a friend who was a travelling salesman. In 1961 he tipped us a horse for the Lincoln, trained by Eric Cousins, called Johns Court.

My dad and I backed Johns Court ante-post and started to look for horses in the National, to do the Spring Double. We picked three or four. Johns Court won at 25-1 and my dad had the double with Nicolaus Silver, who started at 28-1. Lucky John.

It was through my dad that I became interested in betting and bookmaking. From when I was 12 he used to take me dog racing at Walthamstow most Saturday evenings and I'd have little bets. Then there started to be racing on the television on Saturdays, and I'd have a bet with my paper-round money.

Harry Sprague was my favourite jockey of all time. He was the king over hurdles, and didn't ride chasers, a bit like Jimmy Uttley later on. I'd have three sixpence each-way doubles on his mounts, and a sixpence each-way treble, and dad would put the bets on for me with the bookie's street runner who called in at the shop every day.

The very first day after I passed my driving test, when I was 17, in 1959, I took my gran to the races at Newmarket. She loved her racing and I would organise my day off from work so I could take her to Folkestone or Lewes, Brighton or Kempton. I still love Newmarket. I stand and stare down the Rowley Mile and can't help thinking that, for 300 years, racehorses have been running over this same stretch of turf. I don't know why but it makes my spine tingle. The head-on viewing isn't ideal but because of that feeling it gives me, Newmarket figures high on my list of favourite racecourses. And at least it's proper racing, not like in the USA. In my view, racehorses weren't meant to run round in little circles on sand or dirt. That's for greyhounds.

At that time, it never entered my head that I might own a racehorse myself. I didn't even understand what Royal Ascot was. When we saw it on television, we didn't think how wonderful it must be to be there, drinking champagne in a private box. We just thought: "Silly sods, dressing up like that to go racing. Why don't they put normal clothes on, like everyone else?"

By the time I left school I had already decided that I wanted to work for a bookmaker. In those days the pinnacle of ambition was to be a bank manager and earn £1000 a year. Bookmakers' settlers got about £15 a week, £780 a year, but were liable to be laid off during the winter. William Hill had a reputation for not laying people off so my dad said: "If that's what you want to do, write to William Hill." He helped me to write the letter. I got a letter back asking me to go for an interview at their head office in Piccadilly. Dad travelled up with me on the tube. There was a tiny entrance, with a rabbit warren of offices upstairs. They offered to take me on for £4 a week, which was £2 a week less than my dad was paying me to do the newspaper rounds.

I'd do a morning round before school, at about 6.00am, then, after school, go to Stratford station to pick up the first of two editions of the evening paper. I delivered those first editions on my way home and when the second edition arrived at the shop, I delivered them before rushing through my school homework. On Saturdays, I went round collecting the money. "Where do you live?" the man at Hills asked me. "Stratford," I replied. He said, "I'd better give you ten shillings a week for your fares, then. I want you to start in August. It's a six-day business. You work five days out of six."

The Monday I was due to start was a Bank Holiday. As the personnel department wouldn't be working that day (nothing changes), I was told that would be my day off for that week. So my first day at work was a day off, which was a good way to begin. I started in August 1959, as a tea boy. They put me in the accounts department, under Ron Pollard, who later went to work for Ladbrokes. There were about 14 people sitting there, writing statements out by hand and making entries in ledgers, a bit like something from a Charles Dickens novel.

My very first task was to go round asking everyone what they wanted from the canteen. One woman told me she wanted a cheese roll. When I got to the little canteen, the girl there asked, "Grated or sliced cheese?" I replied, "I don't know." She said, "I'll give you grated." I took it to the woman but she said: "I don't want that. They use the stale cheese for grating. I want sliced." How was I supposed to know? That is my only memory of my first day at William Hill.

After a few weeks I was working for Ron Pollard in the mornings and for George Cortesi, who was in charge of the large telephone betting accounts, in the afternoons. When they moved me to Cortesi's section, the first thing he said was, "You're not wearing any green, are you?" I said, "No." He replied, "Good. If you ever come in here with any green on, I'll throw you out. It's a bad colour." Nuts, totally nuts, but to this day I still don't wear any green.

In the phone room, people sat in rows taking bets by telephone. Betting shops weren't legalised until 1960, so it was all credit betting by phone or letter, which was dealt with at Piccadilly, or cash postal bets, which went to a big office in Scotland.

Every telephonist had a little wooden box in front of them. They'd write the bet out by hand, tear it off their pad, and put it in the box. Me or one of the other boys would collect the slips, then time stamp them and pass them to the 'field' table at the back of the room where a man would read all the bets out to another man, who would record the liabilities on each horse in a 'field' book. At the front of the room there was a blackboard, where the senior boys who had been there for six months wrote the names of the runners and riders. Next to the board was a phone. After a while, I was allowed to write the runners up, but not to pick up the phone. That was a job for a senior boy.

When the phone rang, it would be the Victoria Blower Company, ringing to let us know about any non-runners, then to give us a show of betting, then the commentary, then the result. You'd stand on a little stepladder, with the phone in one hand and a piece of chalk in the other, and tap the chalk against the name of the horse that was leading. When a horse was about to win, you tapped its name three or four times. The first time I did it, I stepped off the ladder and put my foot straight into a bucket of water. You washed the board down after each race, and rubbed it clean with a newspaper, which dried the board black. If there'd been the number of races there are nowadays, you could never have done it.

When it got quiet, at the end of the year, one of the settlers, called Jack Herbert, took all the boys who had started that August, about eight of us, and spent two hours each morning teaching us how to settle bets. He was a great teacher, with the patience of a saint, which was just as well, because he needed it.

It was hard work, but there was a great atmosphere. At the end of it all, there was an examination and you had to score 95 per cent to pass. If you failed, you didn't get another chance; you were out – the ultimate survival of the fittest. Four of us passed and four failed. After that, my wage went up to a dizzy £7 a week. Then eight more boys were recruited and the cycle was repeated.

After the exams, each successful boy would sit at the end of a row of senior settlers and every bet they settled was checked, meticulously, to the penny. If you were a penny out, you were told that it was wrong. You weren't told what was wrong, or by how much it was wrong, just that it was wrong, and you had to settle it again, until you got it exactly right.

They had what was laughingly called 'optional' overtime at least three nights a week but if you didn't opt for it, you didn't last long. The option was to do it, or leave. Hills did a lot of business on the evening greyhounds so you could also work overtime for that, and you could work on Saturday evenings as well, if you wished. That really was optional. I wanted to buy a car so I worked at every available opportunity.

Night dogs used to get quite boring, so there was always an office sweep on the winning forecasts at each meeting, to keep people interested. One Saturday night the boardman, who was leaving, put up all the wrong results – the ones he had in the sweep. Needless to say, it caused terrible trouble because clients were ringing up during the evening to find out whether their bets had won or not, before deciding whether to have another bet. After work, I used to get a tube from Piccadilly to Holborn, change for Stratford and then walk home. Nowadays, I'd probably be frightened to death walking home late at night but you never thought about it then. People didn't attack old ladies to steal money for drugs. There were teddy boys wandering about and it was a rough area but there weren't any muggings as far as I was aware. Most people didn't have anything worth stealing.

Sometimes we took so many bets on the Saturday that we were asked to work on the Sunday. Quite often, we were still settling the Saturday bets on Tuesday. One year Hills offered each-way the first four places in the Derby, and put adverts in the national press. We took so many cash bets that the office in Scotland couldn't cope. They put some of their postal bets in sacks and sent them down for us to settle. We were still opening them five days after the Derby – not much liability control there.

For its time, it was a massive business, with several hundred telephonists and settlers. I really wanted to get on in the company and was always writing to Roy Sutterlin, who was the general manager of telephone betting. By then, I was a fully-fledged settler and wanted to know why the man sitting next to me was on £17 a week when I was doing the same job and was only on £9 a week. I was told it was because he was 20 years older than me. That was the way the system worked. It didn't stop me from writing to Sutterlin, regularly.

I hadn't been working for long as a settler when the job of clerking in the large accounts department came up. The clerk worked on the field book, writing up the bets read out to him from the slips the boys had collected from the telephonists. It was the only way Hills knew what their liabilities were on a particular horse, and if they needed to hedge. So I went home and got dad to call imaginary bets out to me while I wrote them down. I wasn't very good. I just couldn't write quickly enough. As it happened, I don't think I even got an interview for the job because there were people applying for it who had been there much longer than me.

A few weeks afterwards, without applying or having an interview, I was given a job in the trade room, where they took bets from other bookmakers, so perhaps my persistence with Roy Sutterlin had paid off. It was a revelation and it was where my betting education began. There were about 50 phones but, midweek, only about 10 of them were manned. Business could be quiet for long periods and then, suddenly, every phone would ring, as bookmakers tried to hedge bets on a 'job' horse; a horse that was the subject of significant bets.

Sam Burns and Billy Alsford were jointly in charge. They would join in, running around, picking up phones. "We don't want Red Diamond. We're not taking any Red Diamond," they'd shout. Normally, the caller just put the phone down but sometimes, bemused, he'd say, "I don't want Red Diamond." He'd back another horse and then, no doubt, try to back the 'job' horse himself, elsewhere.

It was my first experience of two people sharing responsibility for the same department. It didn't work then and it never does. Billy was a great form-book man who had worked on the racecourse for many years, first with his own father, who was a racecourse bookmaker, and then as William Hill's clerk and, later, as Hill's rails representative. Sam's background was very different. He had been recruited from Jack Solomon, a boxing promoter and bookmaker. Sam had run Solomon's telephone betting operation and seemed to know everyone and everything that was going on. Both Billy and Sam were strong characters and both played a big part in my future success.

Working for Billy, in the trade room, taught me everything I needed to know about running a profitable bookmaking operation, while Sam was later instrumental in my being approached by George Walker, but Billy and Sam couldn't work together.

They shared an office at the back of the trade room, with thin walls and open windows. Sam was still active as a boxing manager and used the office for his boxing work, which upset Billy. They frequently fell out, with one of them storming into their office, closely followed by the other. The door and windows would be slammed shut, and all hell let loose. Closing the door and windows made absolutely no difference because everyone could hear what was being said. People just carried on working as if nothing was happening.

For me, it was a valuable lesson learned. To get the right working ethos, you have to structure a company correctly. You can structure it to create conflict and problems, or to avoid them. So often, managers take the easy way out of a difficult personnel problem, with the result that they create conflict for years to come. The best thing is always to make a positive decision and create the right structure, even if it means losing someone.

*

I soon became the caller for the field book but answered phones and settled as well when it was busy. As the caller, as well as performing the task of calling out the single bets, I also had to calculate, in my head, how much money was running on to the next legs of multiple bets. It could get very complicated, especially if the results went against us and there were a lot of multiple bets with sums running on. I liked it, and I was a good settler, fast and accurate. It's like riding a bicycle; you might fall off a few times when you're learning but, once you've learnt, you don't forget. I can still do it in my head.

Betting shops started to open in 1961 but William Hill didn't open any. He had got it into his head that it was wrong for working men to be going into betting shops, and that the pavements outside would be full of no-goods. Hill also thought that all these new betting shops would need someone to hedge with, and that Hills could get 10 per cent of all the shop business without having to actually open any shops.

For a while he was right and the trade room business boomed but, as chains of shops started to emerge, business tailed off. Eventually Hill's senior executives warned him, "It's either betting shops or we go bust." In 1966 Hill bought Jack Swift's business, which included a chain of about 20 betting shops. Then we started to buy up shops like mad. It was the the arrival of the shops that gave me my first experience of managing people and it was horrendous.

All these new shops needed settlers and other bookmakers kept poaching Hills' staff, because Hills had the best teaching scheme for settling. So Hills devised a system under which new recruits had to sign up for three years, at fixed wages. I don't know what the legality of it was but they all signed up and, as soon as they'd passed the settling exam, they wanted to leave because the industry was expanding rapidly and newspapers were full of advertisements for settlers at better wages than they were getting at Hills.

By then I had been promoted to floor supervisor in the trade room and only worked as the caller on the field book on big race days. There were about 40 telephonists and 40 settlers but the settlers didn't want to settle because they wanted to get out of their three-year contracts and go somewhere else. The only way they could go somewhere else was by getting the sack. That's what they wanted: to be sacked.

They'd get a bundle of bets to settle and they'd mess about, go to the toilet for half an hour, be off sick for a few days, and we wouldn't sack them. In those days I was aggressive, very aggressive. People say I'm aggressive now but I was more aggressive then. I've always been somewhat combative and aggressive, by nature, although people who knew me then say that, as I've got older, I've mellowed.

Some of those young settlers were equally aggressive, so they didn't care. Imagine the frustration. I'd go up to Roy Sutterlin, the general manager, and say, "You've got to sack this little bastard, he's only settled two bets all day." He'd refuse to sack him. So there they all were, trying to get the sack, and I was their manager and I couldn't sack them.

"You can't sack him," Sutterlin would say. "If you sack one, they'll all do what he's doing." I'd say, "They already are." So that was my first experience of man management, and it was a complete nightmare, a near fiasco. I learnt that there's nothing worse than trying to manage someone who wants to be dismissed, could earn more elsewhere, and doesn't give a monkey's. It's just not possible to make water run uphill without a pump.

In those days, there wasn't a system of three formal warnings and you're out but, if there had been, it wouldn't have helped. You'd have given them the first warning and they'd have said, "Can I have the other two now, please?" The only good thing was that, after that experience there was nothing Hills could throw at me that could be worse.

*

I was always pestering Roy Sutterlin. He was a very nice man and about the most smartly dressed person I've ever met. He always looked as if he'd stepped out of a Savile Row tailor's window; he was immaculate, an example of one of the three types of manager I've come across in my life.

There's the type who looks the part. He looks like a manager; he looks like he's doing a good job. Then there's the one who talks a good job. He tells everyone what a good job he's doing and 90 per cent of people believe him. Those two types can be frauds. Then there's the third type: the guy who actually is doing a good job. He may talk it as well, and he may even look the part but the only attribute that really matters is doing it. Roy definitely always looked the part and he was probably doing a good job but, right through my career, since I've been in a position to make the decisions, I've tried to find people who are actually doing a good job. I don't care whether or not they look the part, and I don't care if they talk a good job, just as long as they do a good job.

Anyway, there I was in the trade room, with my Billy Fury hairstyle, weighing 9st 7lbs. That was before I gave up smoking. I could eat as much chocolate as I liked without putting on weight. Not that there was time for eating chocolate. I was working under Billy Alsford, who knew just about all there was to know about betting and what money to take and what money not to take. With one quarter the odds a place and no betting tax, there was plenty of 'live' money, and you had to be sharp.

It was total war between the bookies and the punters. Betting tax really ended the war and, when it was removed again, in 2001, hostilities resumed. "When punters are down, kick 'em," was one of Billy's favourite expressions. "When you're winning off a punter, don't start feeling sorry for him."

Billy's thinking was that we were operating on tight margins, there were hard-nosed, professional students of form out there who knew more than us and, if you gave them an inch or blinked, you'd lose. "Don't be frightened to tell a punter that we don't want the bet," he'd say. If a punter phoned in just before a race started, with a bet you didn't want, he'd tell him he wasn't on.

Billy's second favourite saying was, "If they slap one cheek, don't turn the other or they'll knock your bloody head off." No quarter was asked, none given. His third favourite saying was, "The first time you think you know more than them, you're skint." That was a good one, and so true in a bookmaker's business. It became a favourite of mine, and actually applies to a lot of things in life.

There'd be a horse with five duck's eggs next to its name, never been in the first six, forecast to be 20-1, yet everyone wanted to back it. In those days, people wanting a big bet would use commission agents to spread the money around, so you didn't know where it was coming from. What I learned was that, as soon as you think, "That horse can't win," you're dead as a bookmaker. When 'faces' want it, even if you think it can't win, not only can it win, it probably will.

It's the same today. Barry Dennis picks one as his Bismarck and says he's going to stand it but if every shrewd judge in England wanted to back it, do you think they'd get on? No chance. Billy Alsford had learnt his lessons the hard way on the racecourse in the 1950s, with William Hill himself, and Barry Dennis will have learnt his lessons too.

There's always someone who knows a bit more than you do and if you lay a bet, never assume that you know more than the punter. That lesson has stood me in good stead, although I'm a cynical sod, anyway. I never believe a single word I'm told. I believe very little of what I read, and I only believe 10 per cent of what I see with my own eyes.

William Hill himself was a distant figure. He didn't come into the trade room very often but he happened to walk in on the day of the Dagenham greyhound coup, in 1964. It was a race where only three or four dogs had any chance of finishing first or second. After the previous race, a gang queued up at the Tote windows and stood there placing forecast bets on the two 33-1 outsiders, with a few lines combining the other four dogs. No one else could get to the windows. We were taking forecast bets on the favourites and, of course, why would you be worried about forecast bets that were only going to pay 9-4 or 3-1? The second favourite beat the third favourite but when the dividend was announced, it was almost £1,000. Someone phoned Extel to check that they'd announced the correct dividend, and when they said they had, we realised we'd been done.

Hill always wore a white silk shirt with big, wide red braces, and a silk handkerchief. He pulled out this huge handkerchief, blew his nose loudly and said, "I'm going fishing." And he did, but he talked to the company's lawyers first and the perpetrators never got paid. They were deemed to have been part of a conspiracy because they had jointly blocked other customers' access to the Tote windows.

Recently, I was with Barry Dennis and the subject of the Dagenham coup came up. Apparently, at the time, he was working for a Romford bookmaker who was one of the main figures behind the coup. Barry became involved in the operation to spread the bets around the betting shops. He put some on for himself, with the proceeds meant to set him and his fiancee, Marion, up for married life, a sort of involuntary wedding present from the trade, but Barry never got paid.

Work was never dull. I remember during the 1967 Grand National we were so busy that we had two clerks and two field books. I was calling the bets out as quickly as I could but we were so busy that I started to put bets on Honey End to one side. At the off there was a huge bundle of bets for Honey End, which weren't in the field book. We were putting them in the book during the race. In the end there were an additional six and a half columns of bets and, for a while, it looked possible that Honey End might win. He was chasing Foinavon all the way home. Thank God for Foinavon and for John Buckingham, his jockey. Many years later, I met John at Ostend racecourse, in Belgium, where he was working as the jockeys' valet in an international jump jockeys' challenge. I enjoyed reminiscing with him about that incredible race.

I carried on pestering Roy Sutterlin about moving on to bigger and better things at William Hill but he told me there was no immediate chance of promotion and, in the trade room, it was a case of waiting to step into dead men's shoes. But Roy gave me one of the best pieces of advice I ever received. He told me that the future lay with betting shops, and that I should move into the shops William Hill had recently purchased. I took his advice. The day that Foinavon won the Grand National was my last day in the trade room. The following Monday, I started a new job in a betting shop.

CHAPTER TWO

WHO ARE THOSE GIRLS?

Jenny worked as a telephonist in the trade room at Hills. After I'd been there a year or so, I asked her out and she said she'd like to go to a restaurant. I'd never eaten in a restaurant in my life. People who lived in Chobham Road didn't. The idea frightened me. In fact it was ten or twelve years before I felt comfortable in one. Once we were seated in the restaurant, the waiter brought us a wine list. I knew what wine was but I'd never drunk any or ordered a bottle in my life. I ordered a bottle of Nuits St George without knowing whether it was red or white or what it was. I just liked the name.

Jenny lived in Dartford, in south-east London, and I saved up until I had about £450 and bought a Volkswagen Beetle, which made it easier for us to go out. Eventually, we decided to get married and started to save for a house. Jenny's mother was a very good seamstress and she was making Jenny's wedding dress when, about six weeks before the wedding, she died suddenly. It was terrible. Jenny was crying her eyes out about her mum, and about leaving her dad, so I said,

"Look, let's spend some of the money we were going to use for a deposit on a house to go abroad for our honeymoon, and we'll live with your dad for six months."

So off I went to Thomas Cook; my first visit to a travel agent. The man said, "There's this lovely hotel at Torremolinos, the Hotel Mercedes. You can fly to Gibraltar and our rep will pick you up and drive you to the hotel. Have you got passports?" I had never heard of Torremolinos and we didn't have passports, so we got the forms, filled them in and sent them back. After a while, a passport arrived for me but Jenny got a letter to say that her birth certificate wasn't complete and she'd have to go to Somerset House, which was where the registry for births, deaths and marriages was. When we got there, they asked me to leave the room. When Jenny came out, she was in floods of tears. "He's told me I'm adopted," she said. "It's not true. I know it's not true. He's made a mistake."

We got back home to her dad and he broke down in tears and said, "Yes, it's true." They'd never said a word about it in 20 years. It was a hell of a shock for Jenny, especially so soon after her mother – who turned out to be her adoptive mother – had died. All she could do was cry her eyes out.

We got married on 3 October 1964, went to Spain for our honeymoon, and then lived with her dad. It worked out allright, probably because we weren't there much. All we did was go to work, come home, and go to work again, working as much overtime as we were able to cope with.

Eventually we found a little bungalow for £4,400. We'd saved £400 with the Nationwide Anglia Building Society, so we asked them for a mortgage for the other £4,000. In those days, every building society manager acted as if he was God – you were more likely to get an audience with the Pope. Although lending was their business, lending always seemed to present enormous problems for them. They would never lend as much as you asked for, moaned and groaned about the amount you wanted, then reluctantly agreed, provided you paid half a per cent more than the going rate, after which they put you in a queue for several months. You could jump the queue by going to a mortgage broker. He'd go to the same building society manager but somehow got to the front of the line. What a racket that was. Thankfully, it's very different now.

While we were waiting for the building society to confirm that they'd lend us the money, Billy Alsford told me that Hills sometimes made mortgage loans at preferential rates. He wrote to William Hill with a personal recommendation but it was Lionel Barber, the finance director, who I was called to see.

I found dealing with that man over our potential mortgage loan to be extraordinarily difficult. He made me write out all the details and go through it with him and then just said "No" but told me I could go back to him if I eventually failed to get a mortgage. Not likely; I was never again going back to him.

Roy Sutterlin had signed my mortgage application form, confirming my basic pay, and had agreed to include all my overtime in the figure. When combined with Jenny's pay, it meant that our annual basic wage, multiplied by two, which was the usual multiple in those days, was enough to allow us to borrow the £4,000 we needed but there was nothing left for legal fees, let alone furniture. Just before we completed, the estate agent phoned. Someone had offered £50 more than us. If we wanted the bungalow, we would have to match their offer. Luckily, my dad lent me the money, and enough to cover the legal fees.

We had the bungalow but no savings and a mortgage we could only afford if we both kept working, and working overtime. We lived day to day, buying a small bag of coal each day from the local shop in winter, and just enough petrol to drive to and from work. We watched every penny.

The bungalow had been rented out, part-furnished, to a couple who were roller-skating performers: The Skating Valentines. They had sprayed the walls and ceilings peacock blue, using the cylinder vacuum cleaner, which ended up covered in blue paint. The mattress on the bed was so bad that my father-in-law gave us his spare one. The only floor covering was a rug so threadbare that, when I tried to scrub it clean, holes appeared. To round things off, after a couple of months the cooker caught fire. We had no chairs and no money to buy any so we sat on the floor for four months, although I've still got the folding oak table they left behind. When I had it valued a few years ago I was told it was worth £800.

We had only been in the bungalow a couple of years when Jenny had a nervous breakdown, apparently brought on by the death of her mother and the discovery that she was adopted. She had to go to a psychiatric hospital where they gave her electro-convulsive therapy. The cure was worse than the illness. For a few days after each treatment she didn't recognise me and, years later, still couldn't remember much about that period of her life. For 20 years, she never really worked again. It wasn't a very good start.

The financial pressures on us were immense. I didn't have my car serviced for two years because I couldn't afford it. When Martins Bank refused to lend me £25 to have the car repaired, even though I had never been overdrawn, I was forced to sell it for just £50. We couldn't carry on like that so, after having lived in Dartford for six years, we moved to Wanstead, in East London, which meant that we ended up with £500 in the bank. It was the first time since our marriage that we actually had some money to spare. We bought a dining-room suite and a three-piece suite, had carpets laid in the lounge and dining room, the house rewired and central heating installed, all for £400. Then I bought a new suit. One year later, on 22 December 1972, my daughter Jane, our only child, was born.

Five years later, we had our first holiday since getting married. Two weeks in Gran Canaria at £105 per person, self-catering, with Jane free.

*

The Monday after Foinavon won the Grand National, I went to work in a betting shop in Dacre Street, off Victoria Street, managed by a man called Percy. The idea was that I'd settle and Percy would show me how to run a betting shop. It was one of the first shops owned by William Hill, who had bought it from Jack Swift. I thought it would be a doddle. I thought, "I've been settling at headquarters; I already know more than any of them here." After the first race, Percy gave me a big pile of betting slips and said, "Come on, get going. You take the doubles and trebles and I'll take the singles."

I thought I was a really fast settler but I hadn't settled for quite a while and I was used to settling credit bets, not cash ones. It was different. With a credit bet, if someone has £10 on a 4-1 winner, they get £40 back. In a betting shop, it's £50, because they also get their £10 stake back. I'd been taught to settle in ways that didn't work so well with cash bets so I was totally out of my depth and soon realised that I'd have to pull my finger out, and quickly, if I was ever to be good at settling again.

It was a very busy shop, taking 6,500 betting slips a week, and all sorts of strange things went on. The staff weren't allowed to bet but Percy seemed to bet in almost every race. I quickly learned there was the inevitable regular who'd come up with his winning slip and when you'd find the original and hand him his winnings he'd say, "You've got that wrong. It's not £4 3s 6d." I'd say, "Well, that's what I make it. What do you make it?" He'd say, "I haven't got the figure with me but it's not that." And you had to go through it all again. Of course, it was £4 3s 6d; it was simply that the punter didn't trust us.

Trying to make up for lost time, Hills were buying shops at a rate of knots but there was no organisation. The Jack Swift shops were still trading as Swift 18 months after they had been bought. Jack had been put on the William Hill board as a result of the acquisition and was running the London shops. We'd buy other shops which carried on trading under their old firm's name for quite a while, then the Jack Swift name was put on the fascia. It seemed silly to me.

We bought John Hudson's shops in Hull and Parkinson's in Manchester and they carried on trading as Hudson and Parkinson. They all had their own little fiefdoms and although the company was acquiring businesses, there was no central direction, organisation or planning.

After my induction at Dacre Street, I was made manager of a shop in Balham, at 137 Balham Hill. It was also trading under the name of Jack Swift but everything was different from the shop in Dacre Street. The systems were different, the tills were different and even the betting slips were different. In Dacre Street, the slips had two sheets of paper, with a carbon copy for the customer; at Balham Hill, there was a single sheet, with a tear off section at the bottom.

The first thing I discovered was that one of the staff was helping himself to his bus fare every day. I was there for two years and the tills never balanced once. Every single night for two years they were 50p or £1 short but it proved impossible to stop, or prove.

Of course, people did get caught cheating the system but the ones who got caught were mainly the regular, systematic cheats who inflated winnings on bets or deliberately didn't photograph certain bets. The clever ones were those who went for little amounts or waited for the right opportunity. Now and again, when someone hadn't come in to claim a winning bet, they'd claim it, or they'd work a little fiddle during a power cut when the camera was out of action and because it wasn't systematic they rarely got caught.

At Balham, I had two girl counter clerks, a boardman and a pay-out man called Charlie. I was in my early twenties, Charlie was in his late fifties and Charlie thought he was running the shop. He was a typical South Londoner: heavily built, hard as nails, being managed by someone who he thought knew nothing about anything – me. At that time he was probably right. I was certainly no match for Charlie.

Two or three nights a week, Charlie worked as a bookmaker's tic-tac at Wimbledon dogs and, every Saturday afternoon at about 5.00pm, with half an hour to go, he'd say, "I'm going now. I've got to get to Wimbledon." He would walk out, leaving the rest of us to balance the tills. I couldn't cope with him and his Wimbledon dogs and, needless to say, I got quite aggressive about it. He insisted that Jack Swift himself had told him it would be allright to carry on working at Wimbledon, and that he could leave early to get there. I almost phoned Jack Swift up and told him what I thought of his arrangement. With hindsight, I should have done.

On Saturdays, you couldn't have got another person in that shop if you had tried. It was packed. Virtually all the customers were black men, all smoking, standing shoulder to shoulder, potentially a right load of trouble, but they weren't a bad bunch, not like a shop we had in Clapton, called the Pond. It was a punishment shop. If you got sent there, you knew you must have done something wrong. The customers there were terrible and real trouble the whole time.

It was a five-and-a-half-day week. Five days I'd leave home in Dartford at 6.30am to get to Balham in time to open the shop at 9.30am. The sixth day I left home at 9.00am to start at noon. We shut at 6.30pm, even in the winter, when racing finished at 4.00pm and there was no afternoon dog racing. You'd sit there, just in case someone wanted a bet on the evening dogs, twiddling your thumbs, always two of you, in case there was a robbery, and rarely taking a bet after 5.00pm. It was totally frustrating.

There weren't any big punters, apart from the occasional £100 bet on a Saturday, but the profit margin was tremendous. We dealt with about 4,500 betting slips a week and they were all small bets. There weren't any shrewd punters. Now and then, a stranger would walk in, stand at the back for half an hour and have a couple of £1 bets. That meant they were either Customs and Excise officers, or William Hill security men. All in all, it was a pretty good grounding in how to run a betting shop and manage customers, while cutting my teeth on Charlie.

While I was on holiday, I heard that there was a job going as manager of a better shop in Knightsbridge. When I asked about it, they said I couldn't have that job but they had something else in mind for me. They wanted me to go into shops they'd just bought, show the managers how to do William Hill's paperwork, and so on, stay for three or four weeks, then move on to another shop.

The thing that soon struck me was that every shop was different. They were all owned by William Hill but the shop fronts and interiors were all different and nobody was doing anything about it. There didn't seem to be a shop-fitting programme at all. Managers were pretty much just told to get on with it. I guess that's how empires are built: sod the detail, look at the big picture – here we go, we're buying shops and building a business.

Over the next few years I must have worked in 150 to 200 different shops, in and around London and the South-East, travelling to work by public transport, everywhere from Gants Hill in the east to Hendon in the north, Slough in the west to Southampton in the south. It meant long hours and was difficult but I learned about shops and what made them successful, about good trading locations, and bad ones.

One of the shops I went to was H & S in Church Street, Kensington. It was a really buzzing location. You'd walk down the street, look in Biba's shop window and none of the girls in the shop had bras on. It was the swinging sixties but unfortunately it was the other guys who were doing the swinging, not me. I lived through it but it passed me by. I was too busy working.

Apart from that, what I remember best about H & S was the big man who insisted he had given the counter clerk a £10 note, not a £5 note, and she had only given him change for £5. I checked the till and it was correct, so I started to explain that it must have been a fiver because the till was correct. He didn't seem to find my reasoned argument convincing. He had an argument of his own to present. The man leaned across the counter, grabbed me by the throat and collar, squeezed, lifted me off the ground and growled, "I want my money."

I have never believed that the expression, 'The customer is always right' necessarily applies to bookmaking. In this case, though, where the customer was six inches taller and four stones heavier than me, and foaming at the mouth, it suddenly seemed very appropriate. So I gave him the money. The episode also taught me the meaning of the expression, 'Discretion is the better part of valour'.

After I had been working at the Church Street shop for several months, which was my longest stint in any shop since the one at Balham, I went on two weeks' leave and on my first morning back was told, "You're not here any more, you're in Bayswater." The shop was in Queensway, opposite Queensway Station, and was full of strange people: small-time crooks, wheelers and dealers. One man used to come in every day and ask what the girls behind the counter would like; he would ask them if perhaps they would like some perfume or something they had seen in Whiteleys the department store or maybe a jumper. Next day he'd bring it in. He was a local shoplifter and lifted to order.

Our shop was on two floors. The basement had a back entrance into an alleyway and sometimes the front door would crash open, three guys would dash in, run down into the basement shop, and straight out the back. They were the three-card tricksters who used to operate outside Queensway Station. As soon as the police appeared, they'd dash into our shop.

Upstairs we'd have our regulars and downstairs our bigger punters. There was a swarthy Hungarian called Victor, who was rumoured to have killed someone. He was a big punter and always had big money, which he was said to have won as a professional poker player on boats. He'd bet £300 or £400 a race and had a little entourage of people around him but he never caused any trouble. It was my experience that those types of people, often hardened criminals, never caused any problems because they didn't want trouble with the police or to draw attention to themselves in their leisure time.

Another shop I got sent to was in Porchester Road, where one of our regulars was an Australian guy, and another an Irishman. The Australian was big and a bit of a loudmouth, while the Irish fellow was short and stocky but getting on a bit. One day the pair of them started arguing about the monarchy. Eventually the Australian, who must have been three stones heavier, a foot taller, and 20 years younger, shaped up to hit the Irishman, and the Irishman knocked him out with one punch. It turned out he'd been a professional boxer. Remembering the incident at H & S in Church Street, I waited until it was all over before plucking up the courage to go out from behind the counter into the shop and exert my authority.

There were always arguments in that shop. One day the boardman somehow missed out the name of one of the runners. It was a rank outsider and, needless to say, it won, at 50-1. With the favourite finishing second we immediately had a group of punters insisting, "If you can't win, you can't lose. That's the rules. I want my money back." Those who had backed the favourite wanted to be paid out as if it had won. In the end, we paid them all. That was another lesson learnt. The cost of mistakes is part of the expense of being in business.

I had a couple of spells managing a shop in Swallow Street, near Piccadilly Circus. It was a terrific shop with a very high turnover, empty on Saturdays but packed on weekday lunchtimes and afternoons. People used to come in from the West End, from Bentley's Oyster Bar and the Pigalle Club. We even had a smart commissionaire on the door. He was a nice guy and kept the shop tidy but I thought that having him was a total waste of money.

Just across the street, the bookmakers Dyer and Ashford had their office and they used our shop to hedge when they couldn't get on anywhere else. Dyer and Ashford got to know every plot going, so you had to be on your toes.

I got sent to a small shop in Shepherd's Market and stayed there for several months. Lucien Freud, the painter, used to come in, although I didn't know who he was until one of the cashiers told me. He didn't paint me. Pity. Then there was Mark McCormack, the sports marketing man, who had an office nearby. His staff would occasionally come in, have £100 on something and, if it won, which it often seemed to do, give us a £10 or £20 tip, which was an enormous amount of money in those days.

We had one regular who was a porter at the 21 Club. Every Saturday he'd bring in slices of ham, some cheese and a couple of pounds of sausages, which we had for lunch, then shared what was left to take home. That went on for quite a while until he got sacked for stealing from the kitchens.

Sometimes the door would open and ten girls would walk in. I was so green and naive that I'd no idea who they were. I'd say to the settler, "Who are those girls?" Of course, they were prostitutes and they would come into the shop when the police were in the neighbourhood. You couldn't get arrested for soliciting if you were having a bet in a betting shop and, when they came in, they all had a small bet to ensure they had a betting slip as proof that they were betting, not working.

A lot of big bets whizzed across that counter. It was a high-turnover, low-margin shop, and there was a time when we started taking a lot of forecast doubles and trebles on the dogs, the same traps each race.

One day, the first two in the first three races were traps 5 and 6, and the forecast dividends seemed abnormally high. In those days, there was no Computer Straight Forecast; it was all Tote odds from the track. Remembering the Dagenham coup, I suspected that the pools were being manipulated, but more cleverly. Looking back, perhaps a track bias was being created by the harrowing of the sand. Anyway, everyone was in a panic. Enormous sums were running up on the next few races. Fortunately, traps 5 and 6 came up only once more. It cost the industry enough but could have been worse.

I rang Sam Burns, who by then was William Hill's managing director, to say how dangerous I thought this was, and of my suspicions about the dividends. Sam promptly banned forecast trebles. "Never forget," Sam used to say, "every single night someone, somewhere, goes to bed working out how they are going to cheat or defraud us the next day." He was right and I have never forgotten it.

*

When you go to work for a large and prosperous company, you assume that everything is being done in a professional way. You believe that the people at the top know what they are doing. I was proud to be working for William Hill, and so was my dad, whom I'd taught to settle at home. The newsagent's shop had been compulsorily purchased for redevelopment and he got a job, first as a Saturday settler and then full-time. Later, my dad went to work for a small chain of betting shops in Hornchurch. The shop he was in got robbed, he chased after the robber and got clubbed on the head. Much worse, as far as my dad was concerned, his shop got taken over by Ladbrokes. He hated that. Like me, he was a William Hill man, and he retired shortly afterwards.

Even before I joined Hills, I thought they were a great company, led by a great man. It was the company I wanted to work for. The reality was different. William Hill's business had been telephone credit betting and postal football betting. They had a huge football betting operation and then got into a battle with Ladbrokes over the fixed odds for draws. At one time we were offering 40-1 against three draws and 100,000 to 1 against nine draws. Those odds were far too high at a time when defensive football was in vogue, producing a lot of draws. The pools companies switched to score draws to create big dividends but our odds continued to be for any draw.

A guy called Arthur Wyles, a welding inspector, won £100,000 for £1 on nine draws but, worse, because we were taking business away from the pools companies, the football pools promoters started a campaign for fixed odds coupons to pay the same tax as pools coupons. In 1964 Reginald Maudling, the Chancellor of the Exchequer, introduced a 25 per cent tax on fixed odds betting. The next year, Jim Callaghan, as Chancellor, raised it to 33 per cent. That killed off fixed odds football betting and, as a result, Hills lost over £2.5 million in 1964-65. After one particularly bad Saturday, the company had to sell the freehold of its headquarters building, which by then was in Blackfriars Road, to meet its liabilities to the bank. That same week, Ladbrokes also lost a fortune. It was an example of how governments, if they are foolish, can kill businesses by over-taxing them.

In the next year, 1966, we finally moved into betting shops but there was no structure. It was unbelievable. Ladbrokes, who were ahead of us in buying shops, were already creating a brand, with a company-wide shopfitting style; we weren't.

I must have worked in 100 shops in London and every one was different. Every time you went to a new shop, you had to work out how to use the till. I got sent to one shop in Kensington High Street which didn't even have a camera to film the bets because Hills' stores had run out of cameras. They didn't have people going round the shops to collect the films. Instead, managers were supposed to put them in a bag and post them. If the films didn't turn up, managers said the Post Office must have lost them. Later on it was discovered that one of the managers had a girlfriend in the security department. The film from whichever shop he was working in, never got looked at.

Each manager really was running his own shop because there were no district managers or regional managers. If a manager knew he was going to be short of staff, he'd contact someone at head office who tried to find someone to fill in for them from one of the other shops in London. Staff were being moved all over London, instead of within a locality. Every now and again someone from head office would visit five or six shops but no more than that. Bill Balshaw was in charge of William Hill at that time but it didn't seem to me that the business was being managed professionally.

Eventually they put a man called Tommy Garrity in charge of the shops in London. He had been running the fixed odds betting business and didn't know anything about running betting shops, although he liked the idea of fitting them out. However, every one was fitted out differently. Nothing was ever the same. There was no shopfitting specification and each regional business was doing its own thing.

In October 1971 William Hill died and, two months later, we were taken over by Sears, who got the better of a battle with Grand Metropolitan, who owned Mecca Bookmakers. We had 500 shops by then. Charles Clore became chairman until he died in 1979, with Bill Balshaw and later Sam Burns as managing director.

I had first met Sam when working in the trade room. Shortly after those days in the trade room, he left to concentrate on managing boxers and later became managing director of Burns and Downes, who had a chain of betting shops. When William Hill bought Burns and Downes, Sam returned to the fold, with a seat on the board, became managing director and, when Charles Clore died, Sam became chairman. He then brought Len Cowburn down from Hull, where he'd been running the John Hudson shops, to be managing director.

Eventually Tom Garrity asked myself and a man called Norman Vickers, a new recruit, to be joint general managers for the shops in the south and to create a management structure. We started by looking at what Ladbrokes were doing and asked for applications from shop managers for posts as district managers. When we looked at the pay structure for managers we realised there wasn't one.

We tried to work out a system based on the number of betting slips and turnover in each shop and produced a checklist of the things managers and district managers should do. This immediately brought about wholesale change and was the catalyst for a company-wide structure and pay system. Unfortunately, Norman and I didn't get on very well. We tried to make things work, to reach an accommodation, but we couldn't. It was another example of the way in which a company's structure either promotes smooth working or creates conflict. You can't have two people sharing responsibility. It's got to be clear who is responsible for what, and then let them get on with it.

During this period I also formed the view that executives should not be allowed to interfere in departments other than their own. For instance, everyone always seems to consider themselves better at marketing than the marketing executive; to know how to create a better advertisement or colour scheme or marketing campaign. The more creative the job, the more everyone seems to know how to do it better.

The guilty parties are always those with routine, repetitive jobs, without a lot of opportunity for creativity and, in many cases, either with too many staff or not enough to do. That creates politics in an organisation. It is easily stopped, firstly by the boss firmly telling everyone to do their own job, not other people's, and secondly, by ensuring that every time someone is found interfering, they should either be given more work to do or have staff taken away from them. When you have too much to do and not quite enough staff, you don't interfere in other people's work.

I also believe that recruiting staff should not be the responsibility of the personnel department. Its job is to place advertisements, produce candidates, and arrange the interviews. Unless they are recruiting personnel staff, they shouldn't carry out the interviews, even if they wish to do so. That way, managers take on and get the staff they deserve, not the staff that others have recruited for them. I believe in people being responsible for their own actions.

Running betting shops is not a sexy job. It's boring, like painting the Forth Rail Bridge. It's a long grind but it's the job that area and regional managers have to do, day in, day out, and not other jobs, like designing advertisements, which some of them would like to do to relieve the monotony. That's someone else's job. No, the area and regional managers have to make sure that the same things happen every day: that the shops open on time, with newspapers properly displayed and that all the lights and televisions work. They have to make sure that the toilets are clean and have toilet paper in them, that the fascia sign is operating properly and that there are enough staff for the volume of business expected that day; not too many and not too few. It is the most important job in the organisation, because it is where the money is made but, it can be monotonous. You have to have compartmentalisation of responsibilities so that everyone knows what they are supposed to be doing and you have to stick to it.

By the end of the 1970s I had become totally fed up. We had regional directors in Leeds, Manchester, Scotland, Birmingham and London, each with a general manager responsible for the shops but in London there were two general managers, Norman and me, and it didn't work. So I started to think that I'd leave. I had a friend who had a betting shop in Camberley and we decided we'd buy one or two more shops and set off on our own. Looking back, I can't believe I was seriously thinking about it but I was so frustrated at having to share responsibility.

At about this time, Len Cowburn set up a series of meetings with senior managers. We talked and I told him I was going to leave. He said he was sorry but if that was what I wanted, so be it.

Within a few weeks, quite out of the blue, Hills suddenly acquired about 200 betting shops in Wales and around 40 more in London from the receivers of the infamous Slater Walker collapse. It was decided to create a new region in Wales and Norman was asked to become the regional director. John Probert, who was the regional director for London, called me in and gave me a way out. He said, "I know you've told Len you're leaving but I would like you to stay, and now you'll have London to yourself, as general manager." I'll always be grateful to him for that. He didn't have to do it and it was a valuable lesson to me in not taking entrenched positions when you don't have to.

In my utter frustration I had made it generally known that I was going to leave, when I didn't need to and without any very sensible alternatives. Putting yourself in a corner when you don't need to do so is something most people do at some time or other in their lives. When the only way out of the corner in which you have put yourself involves swallowing your pride, it can be a bitter pill. I learnt my lesson and never did it again.

As my father told me, everyone makes mistakes but clever people never make the same mistake twice. I have always remembered that and tried my best not to make the same mistake twice. Thanks to John Probert, my mistake involved the minimum blow to my pride.

I often refer to this as the 'over my dead body' threat. It should never be said by anyone in any circumstances but most of us in big organisations do it at some time or another. If you do it and survive it once, you never do it again. That was how I came to stay with Hills and, when John moved to become director of telephone betting, I ended up as director of the Southern Region. Lucky John, thanks to another John.

We had five regional directors, all reporting to Cowburn. In 1983, Norman and I were eventually invited on to the William Hill board, although not the others. It was a proud moment for me, and introduced me to Jarvis Astaire. Jarvis, an entertainment entrepreneur, had been involved in developing a chain of betting shops run by former boxer Terry Downes and Sam Burns. Their shops had been sold to the

Hurst Park Syndicate, which Hills bought. It was then that Astaire joined Hill's board. Jarvis was the same then as he is now. A shrewd and very successful entrepreneur, he had his own views on everything and wasn't frightened to put them forward, even to the mighty Sears. In 1981, Cowburn succeeded Burns as William Hill's chairman.

My life was totally focussed on work. Once I was in charge of the Southern Region, I concentrated on shop development. I set up a team and set about it in a structured way, which, as far as I could see, was the first time it had been looked at systematically.

There were about 200 shops in the region and I was only allowed to fit out a few of them each year but I could re-site or extend as many as I wished. Betting shops are a little like newsagents. If you want to buy a newspaper and a packet of cigarettes, to which newsagent do you go? You go to the most convenient one. Generally, punters go to the most convenient betting shop. If you have a Hills shop and a Ladbrokes shop close to each other and ask punters coming out of them why they have chosen that shop, they'll tell you it's because it's nearer for them. So your location is vitally important. One shop can be taking £15,000 a week and a similar shop, 50 yards away, £30,000.

A lot of our shops had room for a rearward extension, so we'd extend backwards, or buy the shop next door to give us a double-fronted shop; things that were fairly easy to do and were often very productive but the opportunities had to be identified first.

With Sears in control, and being on the board, I started to learn about the proper way to run a business. Not in an entrepreneurial sense, not about how to run a bookmaker's business, but in terms of business systems and corporate procedures, capital and cash control. Sears was a conglomerate that owned Selfridges and the British Shoe Corporation. I was always telling Len Cowburn that Sears should buy Mecca or Coral, and I am sure he was telling them the same thing, but they didn't want to. I often thought that, after Clore's death, Sears didn't really want to be bookmakers at all.

In 1981, Colin Marshall arrived as Sears' deputy chief executive and in 1983 he introduced Bob Lambert as our finance director. Bob had been working for Marshall at another subsidiary of Sears. In the future, Bob and I were to become a very close team and best friends. Marshall was just getting to grips with the business when, that same year of 1983, he was approached to run British Airways, of which he made a great success.

Unlike Marshall, who seemed to me to be quite a smooth operator, Michael Pickard, who became Sears' chief executive, was a forthright, tough man who started to shake up the Sears empire. To Pickard's credit, he put us on proper salaries for the first time and introduced a management bonus scheme. Although I was on the board and running the Southern Region, I had been on only £28,000 a year. Pickard put all the regional directors on £38,000. We were all overwhelmed. By 1987, I was on £50,000 with a three-year rolling contract. I understood that this was because Pickard wanted to lock us in to the business.

But it was Pickard, who later became chairman of the London Docklands Development Corporation, who sold William Hill's. He was refocussing Sears, and didn't see their future as being a bookmaker. Instead, in 1988, Sears bought a mail order firm, Freemans. Sears' fortunes were in decline and, despite the change of direction, the downturn continued. Eventually, British Shoe went soles up and, at the end of the 1990s, the once mighty Sears empire was broken up.

CHAPTER THREE
ALFRED AND JOSEPH

A few years after I joined William Hill, they moved their head-quarters and telephone betting business from the rabbit warren at Piccadilly to a big office in Blackfriars. Then, in 1981, they moved a large part of the administration to new headquarters in Leeds, although the telephone credit business stayed in London, for the time being.

A few years after Len Cowburn had succeeded Sam Burns, he decided he wanted someone to oversee what by then were six regions. The obvious candidates were myself and Norman Vickers but Len didn't make a clear-cut decision. Instead, in 1985, he made us joint assistant managing directors with seats on the William Hill board. Norman was in charge of the three northern regions while I was in charge of the three southern ones. So, in a way, we were back where we started. Instead of being joint general managers for London, we were now joint assistant managing directors for the betting shops. It was far from ideal and another case of building a measure of conflict into the management structure.

At about the same time, in the mid-1980s, Ladbrokes, whose results always seemed to be better than ours, were expanding internationally. They had bought Detroit racecourse and, in 1986, had 820 betting shops in Belgium, and had just been awarded an exclusive licence in the Netherlands. Several years later we came to the view, rightly or wrongly, that their good results were dependent on one big Far East punter, but at the time they allowed everyone to believe the results were entirely due to their superior management skills.

Len was trying to get Sears to expand abroad and Bill Abbey, who was Len's deputy, spent a lot of time and money in the USA, trying to identify opportunities for off-track betting. Len was also approached by a merchant bank, who told him that Mecca were negotiating to buy shops in Belgium but the deal was stalling. Len moved quickly. Preliminary discussions took place and meetings were set up with the sellers, Bill Abbey and me. Negotiations progressed to the point where it seemed that a final meeting was all that was required to agree the contract. I was delegated to attend the final meeting, to tie up the loose ends, and secure our purchase of a business with a chain of about 250 outlets and a head office in Liege.

A merchant banker and I planned to fly from Heathrow to Liege to join a lawyer from Brussels for a meeting with two men, Alfred and Joseph, who owned the business and who were brothers. The flight was cancelled and we were diverted to Brussels and then driven to Liege by coach. Inevitably, we arrived late, at about midday, having had nothing to eat and, almost as soon as we walked in, there was a terrible atmosphere.

Our lawyer, who spoke perfect English and perfect French, came from Flanders, the Flemish-speaking northern region of Belgium. The two brothers were from Wallonia, the French-speaking southern region. French Belgians and Flemish Belgians often seem to dislike and distrust each other, with a passion. Alfred and Joseph spoke little English and I couldn't speak a word of French. The merchant banker spoke good French but didn't understand it so well, so everything had to go through the Flemish lawyer.

Alfred and Joseph were completely different. Alfred was a carica-ture of Hercule Poirot, neat and dapper, with a moustache. He couldn't pass a mirror without looking at his reflection and preening himself in it. Joseph, who was clearly the boss, knew what he was about but did like a drink.

At about 1.00pm Alfred and Joseph decided it was time to hav-ing something to eat, so they brought in some ham rolls and opened a few bottles of champagne. The ham rolls came to an end but the champagne continued to arrive at regular intervals throughout the day. The negotiations were very slow, very laborious, all conducted in French and, by the time we'd missed our evening plane back, we still hadn't agreed a deal or got anywhere near it.

At midnight, Joseph slid off his chair, tired and somewhat the worse for drink. After his brother had picked him up and put him back on his chair again, Joseph launched into a tirade, all in French, all translated for us by the lawyer. We'd got a bloody cheek bringing a Flemish lawyer into his house. There was no way he was going to do a deal with a Flemish lawyer and why was he speaking to us anyway? Why wasn't he speaking to William Hill's boss instead of an office boy who couldn't sign a deal even if he wanted to? That was me. We gave up and came out at 12.30am, starving, drove around Liege until we found a restaurant with a light on, had steak and chips, then drove to Brussels and stayed the night there.

I was due, a few days later, to leave to go on holiday for two weeks, so in the morning I phoned Len Cowburn and told him, "I am never going to be able to finalise this deal. It's never, ever, going to work with me negotiating. He wants to deal with the boss. I'm not walking away from it but there is no hope of me completing the deal. If you want to buy the business, you are going to have to come and do it yourself." I added, "I'm not sure we should be doing the deal anyway." I am sure Len didn't want to hear that but I didn't like the look of the business or the set-up. It looked as if Ladbrokes were making good money in Belgium but it was nothing like the UK model for a betting business and my experience of the negotiations had given me a good feel for the problems we would face in trying to run a business in a foreign country where three languages were spoken – Flemish, French and German – and not one of us spoke any of them.

At that time I wasn't flavour of the month with Len. I have always been outspoken and had been complaining about the way the business was run. I thought he had allowed himself to become too involved in industry affairs, having meetings with the Jockey Club, chairing the Betting Office Licensees Association, attending Levy Board meetings and that sort of thing. These activities were very important but quality time also needed to be spent developing our business strategy. I thought the balance was wrong.

The monthly management meetings were difficult. It seemed to me that Len used them to bring himself up to date with the business rather than to develop strategy. He rarely seemed to be in the office but was constantly involved in industry matters.

At about this time, Les Green, the solicitor who dealt with our betting shop licensing work in the North of England, took me to lunch at the Savoy. He was touting for similar work in my Southern Region. Within a few days of the lunch, Norman, then in charge of the North, was given responsibility for all of our betting shops while I was put in charge of telephone betting and marketing, which was a sideways move if not a demotion because managing the shops was the plum job and the one I wanted. I got a letter from Green saying, "It looks like I took the wrong man to lunch."

Two years later, when Brent Walker bought William Hill and announced my appointment as chief executive, the very first letter of congratulation I received was from Les Green. It ended by remarking that the main attribute of a great lawyer was foresight. "I took the right man to lunch, after all," he wrote.

I set to work on the structure of Hill's telephone betting operation, which had never been tackled. We had our main telephone centre in London, with a smaller centre in Leeds, and even smaller ones in Birmingham, Hull, Crawley, Torquay and Taunton, for local clients. I started to close them down, although Len Cowburn wouldn't let me close Leeds or Hull, which was where he lived. There was little or no attempt being made to recruit more clients through marketing or advertising and we were getting 80 per cent of our profits from 10 per cent of our customers.

There was an argument for closing down all the small and medium-sized accounts because we were taking a lot of bets on which we couldn't make money. There was no minimum stake and with the cost of taking the bet, sending out weekly statements and reminders, and taking the number of non-payers into account, it was costing us 50p to take each bet. With an average profit per bet, after tax, of just 10 per cent, that meant that any bet of less than £5 was a guaranteed loser for us.

I concluded that the way forward wasn't to close down most of the accounts and concentrate on the top 10 per cent, because most of the bigger clients had started off as small punters, been successful in life, and become big punters. We needed to recruit the small punters who would become big ones in 10 years' time.

So I implemented a £5 minimum stake, which got rid of 20 per cent of all telephone transactions overnight – transactions, not turnover. Then I started a select service for higher-staking customers. We would eventually come to call it Golden Spurs but, to begin with, it didn't have a name. I put a couple of top telephone managers in a special room and gave them the best telephonists, with dedicated lines for the top-staking punters. It was fairly amateurish but business picked up.

A bit later, I noticed that *Raceform* were advertising their Note-Book for the previous season for £10. They were obviously trying to clear their stock, so I got hold of them, asked how many they'd got – 2,500 – and for what price they'd let us have the lot? The answer was £3 each. So we bought the lot and ran a promotion offering new clients a free *Raceform* Note-book after they'd placed their first telephone bet with us. It got such a good response that we soon ran out of Notebooks and had to approach *Timeform* for some of their weekly Black Books instead.

When I took over, we were opening about 20 new accounts a week.

51

In the first month of that promotion, we opened 1000 accounts. I wanted to advertise on teletext, which Mecca were doing, but Len was opposed to it and I couldn't convince him. What Hills did do, however, was take advantage of the decision by British Telecom to abandon its horseracing results service in favour of an open-market premium rate service. Roy Sutterlin, who had arranged for William Hill to supply BT with the results for the telephone service, negotiated the takeover of BT's 168 168 number for our commercial service. I was asked to develop and launch the service, which we did successfully, and subsequently added race commentaries.

The service, called Raceline, employed about 12 people and, within six months, was making the equivalent of £1million a year. I went back to Len and said that I still wanted us to advertise on teletext but with the added benefit of putting our premium rate telephone number on the bottom of the page, with the runners and betting shows. This time he agreed and, within two years, Raceline was making about £2million a year, at a time when the whole of William Hill was only making about £20million.

*

If Terry Ramsden had had his way, we'd have been laying him bets to lose more than the £20million we were making. Ramsden was a City dealer who had made a fortune betting that the Japanese stock market would keep rising at a time when it did keep rising. In the mid-1980s, he was supposed to be the 57th richest person in Britain. In 1984 he bought Katies, who went on to win the Irish 1000 Guineas, for £500,000, which he took round to the owner in cash, on a scooter.

Ramsden was a huge gambler. When Katies won the Coronation Stakes, he was reported to have won £1million. "It wasn't £1million," Ramsden said later, "it was £2million." He'd turn up at the races with a great big minder called Wayne and, when people asked who Ramsden was, he told them, "I'm a stockbroker from Enfield. I've got long hair and I like a bet."

When Ramsden came on the phone it reminded me of my days in the trade room with Billy Alsford. Back then there was one punter who would put £10,000 on a horse at a time when the biggest bet we normally saw was £500. You can't make a book when you've got someone betting like that. You just have to put it on one side. Billy used to say to me, "We'll put that one on the cuff." He'd pretend to write it on his cuff. It was the same with Ramsden. We had a payout limit of £250,000 and the first Saturday he came on, he wanted £1 million credit and very large each-way singles, each-way doubles, and an each-way accumulator. We gave him about £250,000 credit and he laid the whole of it out on the first day.

We told him that what he was doing was irrational because the most we'd pay out was £250,000. He suggested that we remove the limit. We said, "No, we're running a business. The business is making £20 million a year and you want us to lay bets that could come to £20 million." He was out on his own. He was like the man with whom Billy Alsford dealt. You had to put his bets on the cuff.

You know that someone betting like that often ends up unable to pay. If you are laying them massive amounts on credit and you let them carry on, they'll eventually owe you money. Personally, I don't like that sort of punter; they can cause problems. They are a big worry while they are betting and then sooner or later many of them can't pay and cause more problems because of the losses created by the bad debt. All you can do is keep them under control as best as you can and hope you're in front when they finally fail to pay.

In the end, Ramsden did just that. Altogether, between 1985 and 1988, when he was brought before Tattersalls' Committee for having failed to pay Ladbrokes £2 million, the City of London Police estimated that he had lost £58 million gambling. People ask how you can let a gambler like that carry on when he owes you money. He may have owed us money but we'd made more by taking his bets than he owed us, and I'm sure it was the same for Ladbrokes.

People are always owing us and paying a bit of it. We even had one well-known, wealthy bookmaker who, to begin with, was quite shrewd and a winner on balance but then lost his edge and started to appear in the annual top 10 of debtors, always paying some but never all of his debt. No one at Hills wanted to do anything about it. In the end, after many requests to him to settle, I said, "Tell him he's got to pay or we're going to take him to Tattersalls' Committee." He paid.

Every year, we get knocked for about half a per cent of our turnover. Bankers are really impressed because bad debts represent a much bigger percentage of turnover in other industries. It's not as good as it sounds, though, because that half per cent of turnover is probably three or four per cent of customer spend. Now that most telephone betting is done with debit cards, it's less of a problem but if you give people a chance to do you, they will.

You can spot them even now. Someone will apply for a credit account, supply references, want a credit limit of £1000 and lay the lot out on the first day. When they do that, you can be pretty sure you are going to get knocked. It's obvious. They've opened the account to have a bet to nothing. If they win, you pay them; if they lose, you don't get anything. I am a punter, and when the bill lands on my mat, it gets paid by return of post. If it isn't paid by return of post, it means I'm away on holiday. That's how I've always done it but that certainly isn't how all punters do it.

Eventually, Len Cowburn decided to move the telephone business from Blackfriars to Leeds. He thought it would be easier and cheaper to employ staff in Leeds. I was vehemently opposed to the idea and wasn't shy in telling him so. I said, if you want to go somewhere cheaper, we don't need to go to the middle of Leeds. There are a lot of locations on the fringe of London, such as Croydon or Luton. A consultant was brought in who concluded that, if we moved to Leeds, within five years we'd be moving back again. He proposed that we stay in London. His report was debated, then ignored.

Leonard Sainer, Sears' chairman, asked us about the move to Leeds. He wasn't keen on the idea and I said I thought it was a mistake. Sainer said to Len, "Your own deputy doesn't agree with you." I know this upset Len, probably justifiably, but I have always said what I thought, whatever the circumstances. I work on the principle that if you don't want to hear what I think, don't ask. If you do, I will always tell you.

Our relationship was inevitably strained by this and, when the Belgium deal was finally done, he told me that he wanted me to run the business there, explore the possibilities for further expansion in Europe and work with Bill Abbey on the opportunities he was already pursuing. I was not best pleased. I didn't fancy the business and I didn't want to be in Belgium.

I believed then and still do that it was an easy option for Len. It got me out of his hair and solved a management problem to which, as far as I could see, absolutely no thought had been given prior to the acquisition. I certainly didn't get the job because of my language skills. At the same time, I firmly believe that a boss can't always make decisions that please everyone and Len and I are still good friends.

We had a little celebratory meal in Liege to mark the conclusion of the Belgium deal that May of 1986, with Alfred and Joseph, their lawyers, our lawyers and other senior staff of Tiercé Franco Belge, the company we had bought; about 40 people in all. Some of the guests could only speak English, some Flemish, some French, some several languages, so a lot of thought had been given to the seating arrangements. Our lawyer in Belgium had done the seating plan, with place names on each table.

We've all got our idiosyncrasies and Len's was a compulsion to tell people where to sit. You couldn't walk up to a table at a meeting without him telling you which seat to sit on or, if you'd already sat on one to which one you should move. So Len took a look at the seating arrangements and, keen not to offend anyone, started moving the place names around to ensure that people of similar seniority were sitting next to each other.

After a few minutes, Bob Lambert, our finance director, said, "What are you doing, Len?" He responded, "I'm rearranging the places. They haven't been done right." Bob said, "You know they've been done so that people who speak the same language are sitting next to each other."

Len, gathering them all up, said, "Oh, you'd better put them out again." He then handed the place names to Bob.

*

I don't know why the board wanted to buy the shops in Belgium. I think the only reason was because Mecca had tried to buy them and Ladbrokes were in Belgium. It was not a good move. Running a business in a foreign country when no one at the top of the company spoke the language and nobody in the business spoke English fluently was a sure-fire recipe for problems. The business itself was totally different from that in the UK and, like all betting businesses, heavily dependent on legislation. Ladbrokes may have been doing allright in Europe at the time, but it wasn't long before they started to run into difficulties.

We had bought about 250 shops but they weren't betting shops as we understand betting shops. They were kiosks which opened at 10.00am and closed at 1.00pm. There were no betting shows, no commentaries, no televisions and the bets were all on the tiercé races in France. The bets were put into clock bags by the kiosk managers and couriers went round collecting them. By the time they arrived at the head office in Liege, where the security department opened them, the relevant race had often finished. You couldn't think of anything worse. It was like England before the 1960 Betting and Gaming Act but with kiosks instead of street runners. Even so, Alfred and Joseph's business had been making about £2million profit a year.

Betting shops are all about economies of scale. The more shops you have, the cheaper it becomes because you still need only one head office. So we started buying a few more shops in Belgium; 20 from one small company, then 30 from another. Then a larger chain came up for sale, called Le Jockey, with about 200 shops. Ladbrokes, determined to remain the leader in the market, were also keen to acquire Le Jockey.

It was the last big chain in Belgium so it was crucial for us; our last chance of significant growth in that country. I set about formulating our offer and started making site visits to get a feel for the quality of the shops and their locations. It was a disappointing experience.

I remember driving to a street on a housing estate where one of the shops was supposed to be. We tracked down the street number, walked through an arch between a row of terraced houses and found ourselves in someone's back garden where there was a shed with a sign on it – Le Jockey. We were going to have to pay an average of about £80,000 per kiosk and they were poor. We were damned if we did and damned if we didn't.

It was already becoming apparent that Sears didn't support Len's ambitions for overseas expansion. I couldn't make the figures stack up for Le Jockey but, in the end, Ladbrokes made it easy for us by paying an amount that we couldn't contemplate. I've never been more pleased to be outbid in all my life. I felt totally relieved. Bob Lambert immediately recognised the significance of the deal, which meant that we were doomed to be an insignificant business in Belgium but at least we had been prevented from throwing good money after bad. Lucky John.

Part of the reasoning in buying into Belgium was to have a base from which to expand into the rest of Europe, especially into Holland and Germany, but no research had been done and, when we investigated the legal and commercial situation, it was hopeless. I spent most of my time struggling to make things work and getting totally frustrated. I would go to Belgium on Monday morning and come back on Wednesday or Thursday night. It had been arranged that Joseph and Alfred would stay on for a month, to help us.

The way the business worked before we arrived was this. George Xauflaire, who had been a local tax inspector but now worked for the brothers as the general manager, got into the office at about 10.30am. Joseph and Alfred would turn up at about 12.30pm, since Joseph always slept until late morning. They would pick George up, and go to the Café Flo, by the quayside, for lunch. Lunch lasted until about 4.00pm, when they went back to the office just as the clock bags were arriving. They were betting on the tiercé races in France but the bets didn't go into the pool. They had a pay-out limit of

£100,000. They then carried on the management of the business until 7.00pm or 8.00pm, when they finished for the night.

Every Thursday evening they held a management meeting. It started at 6.00pm and the six or seven senior managers were compelled to attend. I've no idea what they talked about because the business never changed. At 6.30pm the champagne was brought out. The meeting always ended either when the champagne ran out or Joseph fell off his chair. Then they all went home, usually at around 1.00am. This happened religiously, week in, week out. And this was the business for which we had just paid £13million.

Joseph had an Italian girlfriend, the sister of the man who ran the Café Flo. Her cousin, Cordero, was in charge of the security department. I always had a feeling that, prior to our arrival, he was also Joseph's minder. He looked like Mike Tyson: short, squat, thickset, muscular and you couldn't see his hands for diamonds. He had more diamonds than John McCririck, and Cordero's were real. Alfred's girlfriend was a dead ringer for Eartha Kitt, and ran a telephone tipping and results line.

On the day we took over, Alfred said there was something that belonged to him in the safe in his office. I asked him what it was; he told me it was some diamonds and gold coins. "Well, Alfred," I said, "We've bought the business, I can't just hand them over." So I phoned our lawyer, who said it was allright. I opened the safe and there were piles and piles of krugerrands, and a little bag of uncut diamonds.

You couldn't help liking Joseph but he was a strange character. He had two offices in Liege, each with a fridge full of champagne. I think that's why he kept two offices. Two nights a week he'd drink champagne in one office, the other nights he'd drink champagne in the other office. There were some wonderful restaurants in Liege and during those first few months the brothers insisted that we went out with them two or three nights a week, often to a restaurant called Le Vieux Liege, where we always had a room to ourselves. The brothers loved it and would spend a long time choosing the wine.

I wasn't much of a drinker and didn't know anything about wine but I remember Alfred choosing what turned out to be a fabulous Mersault and it's been one of my favourites ever since. I learnt so much from them about wine. They were real connoisseurs. They'd go to France every year and bring young wines back for their cellars. How things had changed since I ordered my first bottle of Nuits St George.

Joseph drank champagne, smoked cigars, and frequently spat on the floor. Sometimes he'd spit on the carpet in the restaurant, notice that you were looking at him aghast, and tell you in French that it was good for the carpet. Since the wines they bought were several hundred pounds a bottle, I don't suppose the restaurant owners minded too much.

I was about 44 then, and outspoken, but the Belgium experience quietened me down a bit. I have always wanted everything to be done instantly but, in Belgium, there was no point in trying to force things through because no one could understand what it was I wanted or at least they pretended they didn't. My idea of going to a restaurant was to get there and eat but I had to get used to a different approach. With Alfred and Joseph, when they arrived they wanted to sit at the bar and drink champagne for an hour before they even gave the menu a thought.

Everything was individually cooked, the meal itself was a lengthy process and, when we'd finally finished eating, at about 11.00pm, they'd call for more champagne. If the restaurateur let them, they'd sit there until 1.00am or 2.00am. Once, when it was late and Joseph asked for two more bottles of champagne, the proprietor said he wasn't serving any more. It was a restaurant, not a nightclub, he said. Joseph became more and more rude until, in the end, the restaurateur told him that, if he didn't go, he'd call the police. Joseph tried it on everywhere.

I don't suppose Joseph was bothered. He often had important government officials in his office. George Xauflaire would sometimes say to me, "We've got to see Joseph at 5.00pm. He's got a government minister coming down from Brussels and wants you to meet him." I would go along and watch while they sat and talked in French for an hour and a half. It was the equivalent of Tessa Jowell, the Secretary of State at the Department of Culture, Media and Sport, coming round on a regular basis, for an hour or two's chat. George would then say, "Joseph wants a quiet word with him." We would leave. God knows what they talked about then.

Shortly after we bought the business, Bryan Robertson, our property director at William Hill, who was a regular visitor to Belgium, tried to persuade me to raise the pay-out limit from £100,000 to £500,000. One of the best decisions I ever made was to refuse.

After we'd been in Belgium about two months, I got a call while I was in England. "Someone's won £100,000." That £100,000, without the limit, would have been £400,000. I called in our chief security officer, the clock bag was examined, and we thought there was something fishy. Joseph, needless to say, was friendly with the local chief of police so I asked him if he'd have a word with him because we wanted to call in the police. Joseph asked me round to his house, which was actually more like a chateau than a house. You entered it through big double gates and drove down a circular drive. In the entrance hall, there was a big American eagle, carved by Red Indians. There were cabinets full of jade and china. It was like walking through a museum.

I went in and the chief of police was sitting there. We discussed the clock bag and the system for filming bets. There were ways round the system but, although we were suspicious, we couldn't prove anything. All we could do was make a fuss, question people, make them know that we were suspicious. In the end we had to pay out.

It surprised me how close business people in Belgium got to government officials and ministers. A good example of this was when we wanted to discuss a proposal designed to minimise our tax liabilities, as part of the acquisition. George took the local tax inspector, a woman, for a good lunch. We started our regular monthly board meeting at 4.00pm, without George, and had been going for about an hour and a half when the door opened with a bang and George appeared. His face was grey and he could hardly stand. He was paralytic. Bob Lambert said to him, "How did it go, George?" George slumped into a chair and gave the thumbs up sign. He picked up a packet of cigarettes someone else had put on the table, went to put one in his mouth and stuck it up his nose so hard that it broke in half. He took another. This time George succeeded in putting it in his mouth and lit it – the filter tip end – then slid slowly sideways off his chair. At that point we abandoned the meeting.

When we bought the Belgian business, it was making about £2million a year. In the first year we had it, it made £1.2million and the next year £700,000. The William Hill board was very unhappy. "Why can't you get the profits up? What about taking bets on football or other sports?" The answer was, "Because it's illegal." I explored the possibilities of betting on the Grand National and on Belgian racing, and of installing fruit machines, but it was no good. They were all illegal, with no chance of the law being changed for the benefit of a foreign company. It taught me the lesson that William Hill should never set up abroad because you cannot beat the home team, particularly in a business so heavily dependent on legislation.

Some of our major achievements at home have involved persuading the government to change the law or the tax regime. What chance have you got of doing that overseas, especially if you don't even speak the language? Belgium has three regional governments, so you have to convince all three if you want to change the gambling laws. Even in the USA, Ladbrokes ran into trouble, and they ran into more in Holland, Germany and Italy.

I ran the Belgium operation for two and a half difficult years. The staff were all committed and tried hard but it was like trying to make water run uphill. The language difficulties were immense. Early on, we recruited Martine Verbruggen, a Flemish lady, as a managerial assistant and company secretary. As well as Flemish, she spoke English, French, German, Dutch and Italian fluently, and could take shorthand notes in any of them. Given my language skills, she was invaluable. Without her, we would have been in an even worse predicament.

When Len said that, if we ever got into the USA he'd want me to go, I told him there was absolutely no chance. While I like the USA, I wasn't going to work there. Several years earlier, I had been to the USA, to a conference in Chicago, with Bill Wilson, the head of our Information Technology department, at a time when we were planning to set up our own teletext system in the shops and also wanted an automatic call distribution system for our telephone betting operation. It was my first visit to the USA, and quite an eye-opener.

Before we went to Chicago, Sam Burns wanted us to talk to a retired lawyer in Boston, who had once had Mohammed Ali as a client. Sam thought the lawyer would be able to advise us about the possibility, and possible problems, of opening a racetrack there. We also wanted to see some automatic call distribution systems at work. They were a revelation. Not only could they select callers and choose which ones to put at the front of the queue but, between calls, the telephone operators were busy doing other jobs. Later, when I was in charge, I introduced a similar system. The story of my life at William Hill isn't one of me thinking of something new but of seeing someone else doing something, and working out how it could be applied in our business.

The lawyer arranged to meet us for dinner at 7.00pm at the Charles River Country Club. He told us it would be a 35-minute cab ride. In the USA, no cab driver ever knows where anything is. This one didn't have a clue. Eventually, we arrived about half an hour late. The club was very exclusive and secretive, restricted to just a few hundred invited members who, if I remember correctly, paid a joining fee of about $250,000, plus $50,000 a year.

At that time, my eating out experiences didn't extend much beyond the Berni Inn. At the Charles River Country Club we sat at a table, served by about ten waiters, and the lawyer recommended the shrimp cocktail. I assumed it would be the same as prawn cocktail, but smaller. When it arrived, the shrimps were pacific prawns, about five inches long, in a huge bowl. Our host told us that he didn't think we had any chance of obtaining agreement to a racetrack with off-track betting. Boston was controlled by the Irish, he said, and one influential man ran all the dog tracks. What he said, went, and he would never allow off-track betting on horseracing.

So we flew on to Chicago, to the Regency Hyatt Hotel, on the waterfront. The hotel consisted of a series of towers, with an enormous atrium inside the entrance, complete with a lake, a bridge, a pagoda, and a string quartet that played 24 hours a day.

One day, returning from a Japanese restaurant, where geisha girls washed your hands and face and cooked in front of you, which the waitresses don't do in Berni Inns, Bill Wilson and I got into the lift to go to our rooms. A very attractive black girl stepped in with us and, as soon as the doors closed, she pulled her blouse open and said, "Anybody want to do some business?" My chin passed my ankles. I couldn't even speak. I think I was lost in admiration. I got out at my floor, leaving Bill in the lift on his own with her. When I got to my room, I rang Bill. His phone took an age to be answered. We certainly had a good laugh about it.

And another on our final day in Chicago, when we went to Sportsmans Park racetrack. After watching a few races, we got into a taxi to go back to our hotel before setting off for the airport. As soon as we got in, the taxi driver asked for our shoes. He wouldn't take us back to Chicago until we handed them over. Evidently passengers had a habit of jumping out and running off without paying. So Bill and I both took our shoes off and handed them to the driver. People talk about losing a shirt to a bookmaker but at least bookmakers don't ask for your shoes, as well.

Anyway, in the end Sears made it clear that, although they'd let Len buy into Belgium, they didn't want us to expand into Germany or the USA, so the overseas strategy, insofar as there was one, had nowhere to go. Perhaps they were already thinking about selling us.

CHAPTER FOUR
"GEORGE WALKER HERE."

I was managing Belgium when, in 1987, the telephone credit business was moved to Leeds and early in 1988 Len Cowburn started to press me to move there, which I resisted. I told him that, in my view, all the signs were that, probably not before too long, Sears would sell William Hill to Ladbrokes or Corals or Mecca and, when they did, the first people to go would be Hills' top managers.

I'd lived in London all my life. All my roots and Jenny's roots were there. I didn't want to move 200 miles to Leeds and risk being out of a job, 200 miles from London, where my only chance of getting another job in the betting industry would lie. In any event, it was far from clear that I needed to be in Leeds. Apart from the recently launched Raceline service, I had no responsibility for any of our UK operations and flights to Belgium were much less frequent from Leeds than from London.

Eventually, Len wrote to me. We exchanged a few letters and in the end he told me that he wanted to get me more involved in the UK once more, taking on marketing and eventually telephone betting.

He'd get someone else to run the Belgium business and Sears weren't about to sell William Hill. I was faced with a stark choice: either relocate to Leeds or be made redundant. So I relented and, in August 1988, bought a house in Yorkshire for more than I could really afford. It's the same one I live in now.

Once again, I was in charge of marketing. At the time we didn't have a public relations person on the racecourse and one of my tasks was to recruit someone. I interviewed several people and came to the conclusion that Gay Kelleway would be the right person for the job. The previous year, she had become the first woman to ride a winner at Royal Ascot when Sprowston Boy won the Queen Alexandra Stakes. Gay had since retired from race riding. I suggested to Len that he should see her to decide if he agreed with me. An interview was arranged.

A few days before the interview, Len phoned and told me he'd have to cancel the interview because we weren't taking anyone on. I asked him why not and he said he wasn't able to say but, in time, I'd understand. Then, in November, I got another call from Len. He needed to see me the following evening in London. We went to a restaurant and he told me that Hills, who had announced poor results for the previous year, was being sold to Grand Metropolitan for £331 million. Grand Met owned Mecca Bookmakers and Bob Green, Mecca's managing director, was going to be chairman of the merged company. He'd promised Len that Len would be deputy chairman and Len felt sure that they would want to keep Hills' good people, including me.

At this time Ladbrokes had about 1800 shops in the UK and Ireland, while both Hills and Corals had about 900. Mecca had almost 850 shops, so the merger posed a threat to Ladbrokes' supremacy.

In December, on the day the deal was being finalised, we were called to a meeting at Sears and asked, as William Hill directors, to approve a tax scheme designed to mitigate capital gains tax due on the disposal. We all had reservations but a taxation lawyer advised us that the scheme was proper and legal and that it was our duty to act in the best interests of the company. There was therefore no good reason not to sign, especially since, if we didn't, they could simply remove us from the board and appoint directors who would sign. On the basis of the legal advice we had received, we all signed.

Geoffrey Maitland-Smith, Sears' chairman, saw us all individually for a few moments and, when my turn came, told me that, in appreciation of my 30 years of loyal service, they were going to give me a year's salary as a leaving bonus. Within a week, Bob Green had called a meeting in the Leeds boardroom. Bob had already been reported in the press as saying that Mecca had the best management team, the best technology, the best marketing and the best shopfitting style but William Hill had the best brand name. He opened the meeting by repeating that opinion. They would, therefore, probably keep our name, although they hadn't yet decided whether or not to change it from William Hill to Hills. Bob didn't explain how, if Mecca was best at everything, William Hill had the best brand name.

Mike Smith, who had just joined Mecca from another subsidiary of Grand Met, was chief executive, with Bob Green the chairman. It was rumoured that Grand Met weren't overly happy with the independent way Green had been running Mecca and that Mike had been brought in, as a Grand Met career man, to eventually take control of the business. Smith told the William Hill management that there were going to be redundancies from both Hills and Mecca. One third of the new management team would be from Hills, one third from Mecca and one third would be new recruits. That was their big corporate plan and to me it was bizarre.

That anyone could think that the way to get the best out of a business in the tumultuous situation of such a big takeover was to suddenly bring in a lot of new people who knew nothing about the two businesses astounded me. You couldn't think of a better way to create problems. In my all too frequent experience, takeovers are difficult and traumatic at the best of times and it seemed to me that Grand Met's approach would only exacerbate the situation and cause chaos. If new blood was necessary, it was definitely not the time to inject it. It was something that ought to be done later, preferably in stages, and certainly after the existing management teams had been successfully merged.

The new leaders started to take groups of senior managers, a dozen at a time, out to dinner, at a local Berni Inn, to tell us about their plans. Most of it was superficial, low-level stuff, the sort of ideas that people who don't understand betting shops have: that they were going to concentrate on speciality bets rather than win bets, because of the higher margins; that they were going to get a lot more women into the shops – but not how they were going to do it, or why they hadn't managed to do it previously at Mecca.

Those of us at the dinner I attended left in a despondent mood. We all felt that the meeting had been a sham. They didn't really want to discuss their views; they just felt that they ought to go through the motions, and take us out to dinner.

While Mike Smith finalised his plans, Hills' management were told not to take any decisions about running the business. They weren't talking to us and it was pretty obvious to me and others at the top of William Hill that they were going to get rid of all of us, despite the fact that Len was doing his best to see that we'd be allright. However, that was the last thing he was in a position to ensure. Bob Green was the new chairman and Mike Smith the new chief executive, and it was clear to me that they would be making the decisions.

Bob Lambert suggested that we should get independent legal advice about our situation. He felt there was no point in each senior manager paying separately for advice, so we discussed it with about six managers and proposed sharing the cost. Everyone agreed except Norman Vickers; he wanted to think about it. Bob and I both thought, "They're talking to him." The next day, Vickers said he didn't want to be involved: he didn't think it was right to be ganging up to get advice.

A few days later, Bob saw Vickers strolling up the road in deep conversation with Mike Smith. To me, that was confirmation that I would be out, because they wouldn't want two operations men. Bob wrote a detailed briefing paper outlining our situation and we went to see a solicitor called Peter Cherry, who was a partner at Booth & Co., in Leeds. He was one of the better lawyers I have come across. People will tell you that this legal firm is a good firm, or that firm is a good firm. In my view, it isn't the firms that are good, it's the individual partners. If you get the right partner, it doesn't matter for which firm they work. You can go to one of the top firms and get someone who isn't suitable, go back to the same firm and get someone who is.

Cherry explained what was the best we could expect. He advised us that our three-year rolling contracts would not necessarily be honoured. We had a duty to mitigate our loss and seek work, and Mecca could reduce the payments accordingly. Shortly after the takeover, I made one last trip to Belgium to make my goodbyes and introduce Charles Clifton as the managing director of Mecca's overseas operations. At that time, Mecca were working to get businesses launched in Malaysia and South Africa.

We returned to work after Christmas 1988 and still weren't supposed to be taking any decisions. I wrote to Mike Smith a couple of times to tell him that decisions were needed about this and that but got no reply and he never returned my calls.

*

Early in January 1989, Mike Smith walked into my office and said, "Happy New Year." He was sorry they hadn't found time to talk to me but that was because they didn't need me and I was to leave the following week, on 13 January. He only asked me one question – what did I think they should do with the Belgium business? I told him that it was a waste of time, and had been ever since we had bought it. They should sell it. They did, to Corals for £10million; God knows how.

About eight months later Mike Snapes, Corals' managing director, phoned and asked what I could tell him about the business. I told him to sell it. "We should have talked to you before buying it," he said.

Eventually, they sold it, cheaply, to the Belgium PMU. Mike Smith went through my leaving package with me. It was generous and better than Grand Met were legally obliged to offer. Mike then walked down the corridor to Bob's office and told him he wasn't wanted, either. There was nothing wrong with that. On the contrary, the way they dealt with it was dead right and very professional. Sears had put us on a three-year rolling contract and Grand Met said they'd pay us three years' salary, which was better than we had been advised to expect. The lesson I learnt was that if you are going to get rid of people, do it quickly and look after them properly.

Grand Met proposed to pay us 60 per cent of the money on the day we left and the other 40 per cent six months later, provided we weren't working for any of their major competitors and had not divulged information about the takeover or the bookmaking business. It was perfectly reasonable, more than reasonable, but I had just moved to Leeds, where I didn't want to be, had a £120,000 mortgage and no job and no hope of getting a similar one. All I'd known was working in the betting business. I'd worked for Hills for almost 30 years. Who was going to employ me? Hills didn't want me, and Ladbrokes and Corals didn't need any senior managers.

Jenny got very worried but I'd got the one year's salary Sears had promised, which was £50,000 before tax, and the first instalment of money from Grand Met, so I paid off most of the mortgage. Without a job, the situation still wasn't great, particularly since the house, a large, white, ranch-style building, needed a good deal of money spent on it.

During the interval between Hills being taken over and me being made redundant, I'd already suggested to Bob Lambert that, if we were made redundant, we might set up our own business. Bob had joined Hills as finance director after Sears bought us but I hadn't had many dealings with him. We had had a few arguments over the Belgium operation but got on allright and I admired him as a finance man.

I had overseen the setting up of Hills' Raceline telephone service the previous March and it was already making a lot of money without having the most advanced equipment. I thought there was an opening to offer something a bit better. Bob was in a different position to me because there was always a demand for accountants. He said that he wouldn't normally be interested in my proposal but there were special circumstances. His wife was ill and he wanted to be able to spend time at home with her, which running his own business would enable him to do. We shook hands and our partnership, which would lead to great success for both of us, was formed.

As soon as we were made redundant, I set to work on a business plan. Three or four weeks later, I got a phone call from Howard Perlin, one of Sears' directors who later became chairman of SIS. He said he was very sorry that I had been made redundant and asked what I intended to do. I said that it had been a bit of a shock and that, at that moment, I didn't know. Then he asked, "How well do you get on with Bob Lambert?"

As it happened, Bob was with me, working on the plan. "Yes, I get on allright with him," I said. "Why do you ask?" Howard replied, "Oh, just something I was thinking about. I'll give you a ring in a few days." I said to Bob, "What a strange call."

The next day, Bob phoned. "Guess what? Howard Perlin's just rung and asked how well I get on with you." A few days later, Howard rang again and raised the subject of Raceline. Sears were thinking of doing something along similar lines. "Can you do that?" I asked him. "You've just sold the business." He said, "Yes, the one thing the contract doesn't prevent us from doing is a telephone information service. We can't do bookmaking, but that isn't bookmaking."

Since Raceline looked as if it would make an annual profit of over £2 million on a capital outlay of only £3 million in its second year, they realised, as Bob and I had, that it was a business with a bright future. Howard asked me if I had thought about it. "Not really," I replied, playing for time. Later, Bob and I talked and agreed we had to tell Howard that we were already working on the same idea and drawing up a business plan. We phoned him and arranged to meet in London. He asked where we'd got to with the plan. We told him that we were in the process of developing a business plan, to the stage where we could seek capital from investors, to launch a new business. He wanted to know if the system could be applied to businesses other than racing; to different parts of Sears' business, and asked if we would be prepared to investigate and write a business report for them, for which they'd pay.

We asked to have a few minutes on our own. Since neither of us was earning anything, we quickly agreed that we'd do it but didn't know how much to ask for. We decided to ask for £10,000. Howard blanched a bit. Well, he blanched quite a lot and went to see Michael Pickard. When he came back he said Michael had said, "Ten grand's a bit rich but allright." Deal done; our first. We were in business and earning money.

On the drive back to Yorkshire, we stopped off at a Little Chef and had one of their Big Breakfasts. I said to Bob, "This is our first corporate meal. Keep the bill." We set up a company called Lambert Brown, got a VAT number and sent Sears an invoice for £10,000. At the end of the year we put the bill from the Little Chef in as an allowable expense. The taxman disallowed it because we'd spent the £10 on ourselves, without anyone else present. If you don't ask, you don't get, and sometimes when you do ask, you still don't get.

I carried on working on the business plan for a rival service to Raceline while Bob started work on Sears' report, investigating how the equipment might be used for other businesses. We brought in Bill Wilson, who had set up the IT department and built the telephone system at Hills and who had also been made redundant. Then, out of the blue, one Sunday evening late in January, I got a phone call.

"Is that John Brown?"

"Yes."

"George Walker here."

"George Walker?"

"George Walker of Brent Walker."

"Oh, yes."

"I'm phoning from the South of France. We've never met but Sam

Burns has put me on to you. I've just bought 119 shops from Grand Met. I'm taking them over tomorrow morning and I want you to run them for me."

"I'm already working on something, George. I'm setting up a business with a friend."

"Sam told me that you were out of work."

"Well, I am out of work but I'm setting up this business."

"When are you setting it up?"

"We hope to start in eight or nine months' time."

"Right. Will you come and work for me for those nine months?"

"Have you got a head office for those shops?"

"No."

"Have you got any security systems set up?"

"No."

"Have you got any relief staff?"

"I don't think so. Just the staff in the shops."

"I can't come and work for you, George, but I'll give you some advice. Don't take the shops over tomorrow. You need a bit of time to get yourself organised."

"Well, what about you coming down to London to see me tomorrow?"

"I'm doing something else."

He was very persuasive. So I got on the train and went to George Walker's office in Knightsbridge.

You couldn't help but like and admire George. He was charismatic. He and his younger brother Billy had been well-known East End boxers in the 1950s and 1960s, and George's face told the story. Once a porter at Billingsgate fish market, George had opened a nightclub called Dolly's while Billy – 'The Blond Bomber' – who had fought Henry Cooper for the British Heavyweight title in 1967, ran the Uppercut Club. George had also run a fast-food chain – Billy's Baked Potato – probably the first fast-food chain in the country, and had bought Hackney and Hendon greyhound stadiums. Hendon was eventually sold to become part of the Brent Cross shopping centre.

It wasn't unusual for boxers to get involved in bookmaking. Sam

Burns, the former managing director of William Hill, who had rec-ommended me to Walker, had been a promoter and managed Terry Downes, once the British Middleweight champion, and had betting shops with him.

George loved doing deals and his company, Brent Walker, owned an assortment of businesses, including casinos, pubs and clubs, the Brighton Marina and the Trocadero in Piccadilly, as well as film pro-duction and distribution companies. In the 1980s, banks were falling over themselves to lend money to George's company and he always seemed to have new projects on the go.

I got to his office in Knightsbridge and he said, "I've got to have some help. You're going to have to do it for me." There was something about him. You felt enthused from meeting him. I said I'd help for a minimum of three days a week, for £600 a day, plus any reasonable hotel costs. George said there was no problem on the fees but he would put me up in a flat that Brent Walker owned. I thought, "Sod it, I should have asked for £700." The flat turned out to be a magnificent suite above what used to be the Playboy Club in Park Lane.

I came out and thought, "Six hundred pounds a day, three days a week, that's £90,000 a year, plus a Playboy penthouse apartment." Maybe redundancy wasn't so bad, after all. I talked to people I knew to find out about the 119 shops Grand Met had sold to George; some of them Hills shops and some of them Mecca shops. The Monopolies and Mergers Commission were looking into the takeover and Grand Met had sold the shops, hoping to head off a referral. Of course, they'd got rid of the worst shops: every shop they could find with one problem or another.

So I phoned Mike Smith at Grand Met, explained the situation and asked if my helping George with the shops they'd sold him breached the agreement covering the payment of the final 40 per cent of my redun-dancy money. Yes, he said, it does; you can't do it. So I spoke to George, who spoke to Bob Green, who said he had no problem with it. I should think he was rubbing his hands with glee at getting rid of those shops and that anything I could do to help George finalise the deal suited him.

Soon after that, Green left Grand Met for the USA, where he set up Greenwood Racing and bought Philadelphia Park racetrack, leaving Smith in charge of William Hill. On paper, one of the shops George had bought stood out like a jewel. It was taking a lot of money at a high margin and with a low rent. I went to see this jewel in the crown. It was at Stonebridge Park, near Wembley, one of the worst areas for crime and drugs in London. When some SIS engineers visited the shop to repair a satellite dish, all the wheels disappeared from their van while they were working. I gathered information and drew up a list of things we needed. I got someone to go round every shop on a motorbike, taking pictures of each one. I'd never seen so many poor shops in my life.

The deal between George and Grand Met was a complicated one, involving an exchange of pubs and betting shops, plus a substantial cash payment from Grand Met to Brent Walker. The code name for the transaction was 'Fair Deal'. As far as the betting shops were concerned, it didn't look very fair to me. The takeover was put back and I briefly became involved in negotiating detailed points about equipment and staff and liabilities for outstanding bets.

It seemed to me that Grand Met were taking advantage of Brent Walker's lack of experience with betting shops, and I was able to save them several hundred thousand pounds. I contacted Ted Simpson, a retired accountant who had worked with me at William Hill, and he helped me prepare forecasts and budgets. They showed that, if we ran the shops very tightly, we might just make £1.5million profit, provided there were no unforeseen problems. I told George and gave him a detailed budget, shop by shop. Later, he told me that he used the figures to improve the terms of the deal.

The delayed takeover enabled me to put a proper administrative structure in place. I started to recruit line managers and staff. It wasn't difficult. With Grand Met having started their purge, we were spoilt for choice, with plenty of William Hill's staff looking for work. The key recruits were Mick McGovern, John Dimmock and Chris Shine. After a few weeks I went to see George and told him that, on reflection, £600 a day was too much, when I was working three days a week for him, every week, and he was providing my accommodation. Five hundred pounds a day was more like it. He didn't say, "No, we'll keep it at £600." He probably thought I was mad. So did I after I'd walked out of his office.

George asked me to take on a man from Brent Walker called Leo, who had run some of his casinos for him. I didn't understand why Leo was still working for Walker but he seemed to be a mentor of George's son, Jason. His speciality was making a nuisance of himself. He was excellent at that; there was no one better.

When we were planning to fit out some shops, Leo came up with his own contractor. My plan was going to cost £20,000 a shop and his about £60,000. I said, "Leo, we can't afford that." He replied, "George will want it done properly. I know my George." I told him, "You don't know what you're talking about. The shops are so poor we can't afford that kind of money."

I phoned Sam Burns and told him I couldn't carry on like that. The next thing, I was up in front of George, with Leo there. "What's the problem?" asked George. I said, "Either I'm running it or he's running it." George replied, "Well, John, you're running it." Then he turned to Leo and said, "And you do as you're told." It didn't solve the problem, though. I was still lumbered with Leo, who decided he'd turn his attention to the rents. About a third of the shops had flats and a lot of them were empty. So Leo busied himself finding tenants and collecting the rents.

We needed an office to run the business from and to set up a telephone service. Before I could start looking, Leo told me, "I've found a building. I've spoken to George about it and we're going to buy the freehold." I said, "I haven't seen it yet." Leo replied, "No, but George is happy and Billy's business is on the floor below." That was George's brother, Billy. So Brent Walker bought the building, in a street near Hatton Gardens. Leo drew up a plan giving himself a very big office and everyone else a small one. So we had another row about that and he ended up with an office the same size as everyone else's.

When it came to designing a fascia sign with Brent Walker's name on it, we chose a really loud design: a combination of blue, red, orange and green. Jim Cremin of the *Racing Post* wrote that, when pilots approached Heathrow, they'd be able to use our King's Cross shop as a beacon. That was another awful shop. It had been Mecca's, had terrible lease problems and was always full of drunks and vagrants, there to keep warm.

Jim said to me, "It's not very tasteful, is it?" I said, "Look, Jim, when you are William Hill you can be tasteful; when you're Brent Walker and you've only got 120 shops, you aren't into being tasteful, you're into being noticed." The shop fronts may not have been tasteful but they were noticed. In the end, we launched the business with a pretty strong group of people, led by Mick McGovern, who really understood the business and, like me, was determined to show Grand Met that we could make money from those shops.

I had budgeted for a profit of £1.5million in the first year and that was exactly what we made. I was very proud of that, because they were terrible shops. You couldn't find one that didn't have a problem. Either the lease was running out, or the rent was too high, or the landlord was awkward, or they were in areas where there was a drugs problem. If you found one which didn't seem to have a problem, you knew that it was there but that you just hadn't found it yet.

*

While I was working for George Walker, Bob Lambert was working away on the Sears project. When the plan was ready, we went to see Howard Perlin. They were sufficiently enamoured to say they wanted Bob and me to set up the business. We negotiated an agreement under which, at the end of five years, if profit targets were met, we would each receive a substantial payment. It all took several months and we were getting to the stage where I was going to have to tell George Walker that the time had come for me to leave.

We'd launched the betting shop business in April and, since then, I'd rarely seen or heard from Walker although he had telephoned on day one.

"Everything open?"

"Yes."

"Everything going allright?"

"Yes."

"Thanks very much." That was the end of the conversation.

By late July I was still working three days a week for him and decided I'd leave at the end of September. I went to see George.

"George, I'm going to be leaving you at the end of September."

"You can't do that."

"I'm going to do it. I told you."

"No, you can't do it."

Then George suddenly said, "I need to confide in you. I've bought William Hill."

"What do you mean, you've bought William Hill?"

"I've bought it, lock, stock and barrel."

"What have you paid for it?"

"£705 million."

"Oh my God, George. That seems a lot."

"I've got the figures," said George. "They've told me it's going to make £58 million this year and £70 million next year, so it's only 10 times my first year's projected profit. I want you to run it."

"George, I've told you. Bob Lambert and I are setting up a business together."

"Well," said George, "he can come and be finance director."

George produced a single sheet of paper. It said that Grand Met agreed to sell William Hill to Brent Walker for £705 million, provided that, by early September, Brent Walker produced evidence of their ability to fund the purchase and that the deal was completed by the end of December. A payment of £50 million was to be deferred for a year. The document had been signed by George Walker and Sir Allen Shepherd, Grand Met's chairman. Grand Met were committed – if George could deliver.

Bob was away on holiday in Europe with his two daughters but, meticulous as ever, he had left an itinerary and phone number for every location in case he needed to be contacted. When I got home, I phoned him in Luxembourg. "Are you sitting down?" I asked. He said, "No." I told him, "Well, sit down, otherwise you are going to fall down. George Walker has just told me he's bought William Hill, lock, stock and barrel, and I can be chief executive and you can be finance director."

The deal with Sears would have given us both the chance to make some money and enjoy financial security but starting a new business would be a gamble. George's offer was more certain and paid more in the short-term. I also had a strong emotional desire to be chief executive of William Hill. Sears were going to lend us £5million and I was proud that a big corporation had that amount of confidence in us.

On the other hand, there was a possibility we could do a deal with George over Raceline. If we didn't join him and went ahead with our plans, we'd damage the £2million profit he'd be looking for from Raceline as part of his new purchase because we were going to offer a more advanced service. If we did join him, Sears might still find someone else to set up and run the operation. George had to consider that possibility.

I put it to George that Bob and I would be passing up the chance to make a considerable sum and he quickly proposed a scheme that gave us a percentage of Raceline's profits above a certain figure. If Raceline was sold by Brent Walker, we'd be given a sum similar to the one Sears had offered. That made the decision very easy for us, especially when George declared, "I always pay my chief executives 100 grand, and my finance directors 90 grand."

George was an interesting man. He wanted to make a lot of money out of business himself but he was very happy for others to make money as well. In all my years with William Hill before George Walker came along, I had never received a bonus, except when I was made redundant; and I had been given some share options towards the end. George paid people quite well and, as our deal with him indicated, he was prepared to share some of the upside. It was a lesson I took to heart and, later on, it influenced the decision made by Bob and me to share our success with other executives.

George immediately employed Bob at £500 a day to assist with the financial side of the business and deal with the information that was starting to come in from Grand Met. If the sale was to go through, we had to produce evidence that it could be funded. Bob asked me whether Brent Walker had a detailed business plan and I said I'd no idea. I asked George. "What's the business plan, George?" He said, "Oh, I haven't got one. You and Bob have to do that, to support the £70 million profit projection, so we can get the money off the banks."

Walker was friendly with Sir Allen Shepherd and the story was that they'd struck the initial deal in the back of a taxi. George insisted that Grand Met warrant that William Hill were going to make £55 million profit in 1989. They eventually reached a compromise under which it was agreed that, if Hills made less than £51 million then, for every £1 million less than £55 million, £12.8 million would be knocked off the £705 million purchase price, which had represented a price/earnings ratio of about 12.8:1. That part of the deal would become very significant.

Seven hundred and five million pounds was a lot but, like a lot of people during the boom times in the late 1980s, Walker bought businesses on the principle that it didn't matter too much if you paid a full price because, in a year or two's time, due to rampant inflation, the business would still be worth more than you'd paid for it. That assumption was going to be very costly for a lot of people.

Bob and I and Terry Rainback, a senior figure at Standard Chartered Bank, the main lenders, set about producing a prospectus, including a detailed ten-year business plan, to present to a wide range of banks. In the meantime, Standard Chartered and Lloyds supplied a letter of intent, allowing negotiations to proceed. George hadn't told Grand Met about his plans for Bob and me and Shepherd had indicated that Mike Smith would be available to run the business for a couple of years and would then either stay with Brent Walker or move back to Grand Met.

When Grand Met and Brent Walker met to finalise the details of the sale and exchange contracts, at the offices of Simmons & Simmons, a big international law firm, Bob and I were in a separate room, regularly visited by members of Brent Walker's team, led by Wilfred Aquilina.

Grand Met's team, who didn't know we were there, were led by Peter Cawdron. Meanwhile, George Walker and Sir Allen Shepherd went off for dinner together. At the meeting, Grand Met told Brent Walker that they were going to sell 40 of their London shops to Ladbrokes because, following Grand Met's takeover of William Hill, the Monopolies and Mergers Commission had ruled that, where a new monopoly had been created in a particular locality, one of the previously rival shops had to be disposed of. In compensation, Grand Met proposed to knock £20 million off the purchase price.

Bob and I looked at the first ten on the list and they weren't within a quarter of a mile of another of their shops, which was the relevant distance. An hour later, after a long discussion, it appeared that only ten of the forty were affected by the 440-yard rule. It seemed to us that Grand Met were simply selling some of their best shops, which may have had a low book value, in order to give a big boost to that year's profits. Nevertheless, Brent Walker accepted Grand Met's proposal.

We had another long debate about Grand Met's disclosure that there were several bets on future events that could result in very big payouts. There were bets on either Elvis Presley or the Loch Ness monster turning up alive but the one that attracted our attention was a bet recently placed by a middle-aged man, that he would play for Manchester United. This was a middle-aged dreamer with a difference. His name was Michael Knighton and, after placing the bet, he became a director of Manchester United, put on a team shirt, and kicked the ball around the pitch for the cameras. If he had done the same during a match, the payout would have been, I think, £1 million. In the end Grand Met agreed that, if Knighton won his bet, they would pay.

These big deals are always done sometime after midnight. It's a lawyer thing. No lawyer seems capable of doing a deal at 4.00pm; they are always done in the middle of the night, with discussions in different rooms, and hundreds of minor changes. At about 8.00pm, Wilfred called Bob and me into the room and announced to the

Grand Met team that we were the people who would be running William Hill and that we would now join the meeting. Mike Smith looked stunned. Instead of him being retained to run Hills after the sale, it was going to be run by the men who he had got rid of.

Walker and Shepherd came back at about 10.30pm and both of them started to lambast their negotiating teams for not having made more progress towards the completion of the deal, which was finally done in the early hours of the morning. It was an amazing, almost unbelievable turnaround. There I was, chief executive of the business from which I had been made redundant less than a year earlier, with almost twice as many shops as when I had left as assistant managing director. Lucky John.

Becoming chief executive was the fulfilment of all my ambitions. From the time when I had been having a bet with my dad, I'd always wanted to join William Hill and, after I'd joined, all I ever wanted to do was to be the boss. For me, William Hill had been the greatest bookmaker of his time and in the 1950s his business was the clear market leader. I was determined to make the business that carried his name the market leader once more. I was to travel a long and winding road before I achieved my ambition.

CHAPTER FIVE
TROUBLE

A new company, the William Hill Group, was set up to buy the businesses from Grand Met but the process was delayed by the need to obtain clearance from the Office of Fair Trading for the sale of Brent Walker's own betting shops to the new company. The final price was £685million (£705million less £20million for the shops Grand Met sold to Ladbrokes.) Three hundred and fifty million pounds came from a bank loan, £285million from Brent Walker in the form of a high-interest loan note, with the remaining £50million deferred for a year, interest free. Brent Walker were legally committed to pay the £50million, in cash, to the William Hill Group, which, in turn was obliged to pay it to Grand Met.

With inflation and interest rates both very high, Bob Lambert had raised the question of the high level of bank debt that the William Hill Group was going to carry. The interest payments due to Brent Walker on the £285million loan note did not actually have to be paid, at least for the time being, but heavy interest payments had to be made to the banks on the £350million loan. Bob was told by George Walker that

Brent Walker would be disposing of assets to enable it to lend money to William Hill, so that we could reduce the sum owed to the banks. That would have reduced our interest payments and given us more flexibility. In February 1990, George did actually sell Whyte & Mackay, a Scotch whisky distillery, for £160million, but the money was not made available to William Hill to reduce its bank loans.

At that time, the rate of inflation was almost 8 per cent and interest rates were at a record high. At the end of 1989, the bank rate was a staggering 15 per cent, compared with less than 4 per cent in 2003. The rate of interest on our bank loans was even higher, about 2 per cent above the bank rate. Borrowing was phenomenally expensive and George's business empire was built on borrowings. The capital and interest repayments on the £350million bank loan were crippling and swallowed up most of our spare cash. It wasn't a very stable situation to be in, with little or no room for error. We really needed to achieve the projected profit of £70million.

Grand Met's financial year ended on 30 September, almost a month after Brent Walker had exchanged contracts for the purchase of William Hill. Part of the sale agreement was that the purchaser and their accountants would prepare draft 'completion accounts' which would then be agreed with the seller's accountants. In the event of a dispute, an expert would be appointed to give a ruling. The profit figure for the year ended September 1989 would be taken from these completion accounts, which would generally follow normal accounting rules but were subject to particular requirements set out in the sale agreement. The William Hill Group's accountants were Leigh Carr and KPMG, who were also Brent Walker's joint auditors. KPMG were also Grand Met's accountants and auditors, acting through a different partner and team.

Just before the sale was completed, in December 1989, Grand Met advised us that, based on their routine year-end accounting work, William Hill's profit was £58million. Even with the minor adjustments that the completion accounts might bring, the figure was clearly handsomely above the crucial figure of £51million, the figure that would trigger reductions in the purchase price. There was even a suggestion that it was not necessary to produce completion accounts. Fortunately, that idea was rejected. Those accounts were accompanied by a Grand Met certificate signed by the previous management of William Hill and KPMG, as Grand Met's auditors, stating that the figures were accurate and properly prepared and that they would be used to prepare the statutory accounts of the business.

During the three months from September to December 1989, between the deal being signed and its final completion, the existing management seemed to make only a token effort to run the business. Most had already decided to leave rather than work for Brent Walker, took any holiday that was owed, and just let the business tick over.

Bob and I tried to arrange to meet senior staff, which was permitted under the sale agreement. Mike Smith reluctantly agreed but insisted that we were only to discuss our plans for the future, not the current business. So, having agreed to pay £685 million for the business, we were prevented from receiving a briefing from the staff before completion. Grand Met made no attempt to discourage senior staff from leaving. In fact, they offered some of them jobs and attractive termination packages if they left.

Not surprisingly, given our past relationship, I wasn't keen to keep Norman Vickers but Bob persuaded me that it would be best for the business. When we met Norman he insisted on seeing Brent Walker's five-year business plan before considering working for us. As there was no such plan, the post of operations director was soon vacant.

Just as my involvement left no room for Mike Smith, so Bob's appointment as finance director meant that post was also spoken for. Mike Taker, the personnel director, was committed to remaining with Grand Met and his deputy also wanted to return to them, so the post of personnel director was vacant. Terry Probert, the director of telephone betting and racecourse operations decided to set up in business on his own: another managerial vacancy. The marketing director decided to stay, only to resign soon after we took over, when I cut his budget, cancelled expensive plans for brand marketing and asked him to replace humorous advertisements with price-led ones. Jim Dove, the information technology director, had employed a small company to develop software for a new multi-million-pound computer installation. They were behind schedule and blaming the specification supplied by Jim, who was another early emigrant.

We finally took over on 13 December 1989. I arrived in what had been Mike Smith's office and opened the desk drawers to find that there wasn't a single piece of paper in any of them. The filing cabinets were empty and the computer had been wiped clean, yet the contract stipulated that all documents, wherever they were stored, were to remain in the business. When I asked the secretary where the paperwork was, she said there was none; it had all gone. We got our lawyers to raise the matter with Grand Met's lawyers, who replied that it was Mike Smith's style to run a paperless office.

Returning to William Hill was like discovering the *Marie Celeste*. We got on board to find that there were no commanding officers and no navigation systems. The business was drifting aimlessly on uncharted waters. The existing management had been uncooperative and obstructive in the run-up to the takeover and we found a business in turmoil. We inherited shops where the bailiffs had sequestered equipment because of county court judgements for the non-payment of bills. Phones had been cut off. Many of the operations' staff were disaffected because they had been forced to relocate.

One of their strategies had been to move senior operational staff around. People from every level of management had been faced with the choice of either relocating or leaving. Many had agreed, reluctantly, to relocate, as I had done when faced with the same dilemma. There was mail still going to departments in the Leeds office that had been relocated to London, with no one forwarding it on, or even opening it, and the betting shops were short of staff.

Bob Lambert's first task was to produce by March 1990 a set of draft completion accounts for the financial year ended 30 September 1989; accounts that would determine whether or not a refund was due from Grand Met. Bob immediately set to work, using the accounts that had been prepared by William Hill for Grand Met before the completion of the sale, which showed a profit of £57 million. He wasn't happy with some of the figures, or with the processes used to arrive at them. After a few weeks, Bob believed that, if his initial concerns proved justified, the true profit for 1989 could be less than the key figure of £51 million.

A second problem was that KPMG refused to provide a copy of a report they had written about the financial systems operated after William Hill had merged with Mecca. They insisted that these were confidential audit papers. Given that KPMG were still the business's auditors, we found their refusal unacceptable. I telephoned one of their senior partners, Jim Butler, and told him what I thought of him and his firm, in no uncertain terms. It was their report and he was probably entitled to deny us access to it but I believed he was wrong.

These two problems highlighted a third one, which we had not contemplated. KPMG had a massive potential conflict of interest. They had not found a clear way of distinguishing between their duties as auditors, which was a continuous duty to William Hill, regardless of who owned the company, and their separate roles as accountants to the seller, Grand Met, and to the buyer, Brent Walker.

Bob told them that if they ever had to choose between Brent Walker and Grand Met, they would obviously choose Grand Met because it was a bigger business generating bigger fees. The William Hill Group didn't want to be left in the lurch and he urged them to recognise, sooner rather than later, that they had or might have a conflict of interest and that it would be better if they resigned as the purchaser's accountants and auditors. KPMG insisted that they were comfortable with their position and would never leave William Hill in the lurch.

When Brent Walker bought William Hill, KPMG and Leigh Carr prepared an extensive long-form report for Brent Walker. That, together with the certificate on the annual accounts, meant that Brent Walker believed the accounts had been given a clean bill of health – yet KPMG had produced an audit report that we understood was critical of the accounting systems and stated that the amalgamation of Mecca and William Hill hadn't been effected properly. As auditors, they had identified problems yet weren't prepared to tell William Hill's new management what the problems were, to enable us to correct them.

On 12 March 1990, the William Hill Group submitted provisional draft completion accounts supported, in writing, by both Leigh Carr and KPMG. These showed a profit of £44million for 1989, £14million less than the £58million claimed by Grand Met, and well below the trigger point of £51million. The £14million reduction related to around 48 different areas of work.

Some of the methods Grand Met had used to arrive at a figure of £58million would have been comical if they hadn't had such serious implications. For instance, at the start of 1989, they had a wages department in Leeds and another in London. During the year, the Leeds department was closed and the work transferred to London. Additional permanent staff were to be recruited in London but the intention was to reduce the total number of permanent wages staff, to cut costs. By the end of the year, the required additional permanent staff had not yet been recruited and temporary staff were employed.

Grand Met concluded that the labour costs of the department for the year were the cost of the permanent staff in London, not of the temporary staff, nor of the permanent staff employed in Leeds during the first part of the year. The justification was that those staff were not part of the company's long-term plan. The anticipated cost of the permanent staff yet to be recruited wasn't included, either, which would at least have been more logical.

Then they added in additional profits they expected to make in the future, for instance from plans to move into cheaper offices in Leeds, even though they hadn't actually done it yet. It was bizarre and made you think of the dubious accounting methods exposed by Terry Smith in his book, *Accounting for Growth*, published in 1992, in which Grand Met received a mention. During a meeting, later on, Mike Smith actually told Bob Lambert that Bob was an old-fashioned accountant, who didn't understand what could be done to determine profits when acquiring and amalgamating businesses. Thank God for old-fashioned accountants.

Grand Met and their auditors, KPMG, questioned us about the draft completion accounts and, on Grand Met's behalf, KPMG produced their own version of the completion accounts. They accepted a number of the changes we had made – they really had no option – but put forward compensating changes which maintained the original profit figure of £58million. Discussions were held between George Walker and Sir Allen Shepherd, Grand Met's chairman, in an attempt to settle the dispute, perhaps by Grand Met waiving the deferred payment of £50million due a year after the sale. These talks failed and not only was the dispute not resolved but Grand Met refused to refer it to an expert for determination.

It was only years later, after Bob had written to Sir Colin Marshall, his former boss and one of Grand Met's non-executive directors, outlining the case and the executive's failure to abide by the contract and appoint an expert to rule on the dispute, that Ray Hinton of Arthur Andersen was finally appointed to adjudicate. Maybe it was best that we didn't know then that it would take until 1996, and a huge amount of work, to finally get a decision.

Each side made four major written submissions with further minor submissions, with each side providing evidence and arguments to support and advance their own case. The submissions were substantial and complex, with many volumes of documents taking up several yards of shelving. Each one took months to prepare, involved a large number of people, and cost a great deal, with the arguments ranging from matters of lofty principle to detailed cashbook analysis.

We had repeatedly told KPMG that they couldn't act on both sides of the claim, for both Brent Walker and Grand Met, but kept being told that it was allright; they'd erected Chinese walls that kept the team working for Brent Walker separate from the team working for Grand Met. What a joke.

One day, Bob attended a meeting at Brent Walker. Wilfred Aquilina, Brent Walker's finance director, was called out to see a top-level delegation from KPMG. They had come to inform him that they would have to terminate their position as Brent Walker's accountants in relation to the purchase of William Hill, with immediate effect, just as Bob had always predicted, and they had always denied.

Wilfred was incandescent with rage, so much so that they said they would think about it again and come back the next day. Bob returned to William Hill's office and called into the room where KPMG staff were still working, as the purchaser's accountants, on the claim, apparently unaware of KPMG's decision to pull out. He didn't mention what had happened at the earlier meeting, hoping that the problem would disappear the next day.

One of the people working on the accounts with Bob was Jewish. Bob knew that an important Jewish holiday was due to start that evening and advised the man to make his way home in good time. No, he replied, it doesn't matter, I'll stay. Bob, who always worked late, then went to his own office and carried on working.

Acting under instructions from his boss at KPMG, the man's team packed large quantities of sensitive papers containing detailed analyses and reports on the dispute into a car and left. They even persuaded the night security guard to open the locked offices of senior management and took papers which they knew to be there. Remember that the KPMG team were not acting in their capacity as auditors but as the purchaser's accountants. It was not the sort of behaviour you would expect from a highly-regarded professional firm.

While this was happening, Bob was still in his office on another floor. If they had wished, KPMG could have informed him of their intentions. For obvious reasons, they chose not to. The next morning we quickly realised that none of the KPMG team had arrived and that they had left the previous evening with boxloads of papers. We called our security chief, Dennis Burke, and told him to go to

KPMG's head office and make a nuisance of himself and not to leave until he was either removed by the police or had got our files and papers back. Dennis remained there all day, constantly badgering them. KPMG argued that they were their files and papers but they were on very weak ground because the papers all related to work on the claim and were prepared for and paid for by us.

I again phoned Jim Butler at KPMG and this time he got both barrels. Prefaced with a fair few expletives, I accused him of being a liar, a cheat and a thief. When he threatened to sue me for slander, I encouraged him. I told him that the sooner we were in court the better because I couldn't wait to have their behaviour exposed to public view. Not surprisingly, he didn't pursue the matter.

We spent most of that day trying to find a way of getting the papers back and asked our lawyers to arrange for us to see a barrister, Mark Barnes, whom we had been consulting on different aspects of the dispute. Late that evening, we duly met Barnes, and sought to persuade him to ask a judge to grant an injunction to be served on KPMG during the night or the next morning, preventing them from using the papers and requiring their immediate return. In my eyes, it was a case of deliberate and premeditated theft. Not for the last time, the law let us down.

The barrister said it was debatable whether it was theft. Bob said, "No, it's not debatable." KPMG had taken our papers, some from locked private offices, put them in a car, and driven off. In anybody's language, that was theft. Barnes said that, in order to prove theft, you had to show that the person who took the property intended to permanently deprive you of it. In this case, because it was KPMG, they almost certainly intended to return the property. At that point I gathered up a load of books from his desk and walked towards the door. He asked, "What are you doing?" I said, "I'm taking these books." He protested, "But they're mine." I said, "Yes, but I'm not going to permanently deprive you of them. I'm going to bring them back eventually." He didn't find it in the least amusing, although our solicitor, Mark Dawkins, was smiling behind his back.

Then he said that, to get an injunction, we'd have to show that we were suffering some damage that couldn't be repaired in some other way and, in any case, we would have serious difficulty in persuading a judge that KPMG had acted as they had done. He simply wouldn't believe it. It was not the last time that we found that reputation carried weight in English Law, rather than facts. So we gave up on that.

The security guard may have been at fault in not checking with someone before unlocking private offices and in not challenging KPMG staff when they carried boxes of papers to their car but you could understand why he had acted as he had. These were KPMG staff, presumably honourable chartered accountants, and paid advisors to our company. It never crossed his mind that they were about to remove papers without anyone's knowledge or authorisation.

The papers would be very valuable to the KPMG team working for Grand Met on the claim and, given the circumstances, their removal was highly suspicious. They claimed that everything was alright, because they had Chinese walls. If there were Chinese walls and the papers weren't going to be seen on the other side of the walls, it begs the question: why remove them?

On the following day we continued to apply pressure to KPMG. Finally, at their request, Bob and our solicitors went to the offices of their solicitors, where an agreement was reached. They would return the papers, which filled four or five very large cardboard boxes, but keep copies. Crucially, they accepted, in writing, a strict limitation on their use of the papers.

I remember Bob coming back to the office after the meeting, white with anger. He said that he had told the partner at KPMG responsible for Brent Walker and William Hill that both he and his firm were a disgrace to the accounting profession and that, for the first time in his career, Bob was ashamed to be a chartered accountant. For Bob, always a perfect gentleman and the most honest and correct man I have ever met, that was as strong as it got.

One KPMG team had signed off a profit of £58million by William Hill and were working for Grand Met to produce evidence that this was an accurate figure. Simultaneously, another KPMG team had signed off a profit of £44million and were working for William Hill to produce evidence to support their view. It sounds bizarre and it was bizarre but that was the position they had got themselves into and, very shortly, their position would be in the public domain.

Bob and I suspected that they were coming under pressure from Grand Met to choose between either working for them or working for us and losing their worldwide work with Grand Met. Could any firm have ever had a bigger conflict of interest, yet carried on working for both sides for so long? I doubt it.

We will never know how KPMG finally, belatedly, arrived at the conclusion that they had been wrong all along. Was it pressure from Grand Met or fear of public humiliation? Only Butler and his partners know but, having finally reached that conclusion, what they then did, in taking the papers from William Hill's offices, beggars belief. For Bob and I, it was a bitter pill to swallow because we, and Brent Walker, had consistently been assured that KPMG wouldn't let us down and, as a result, we had been prevented from removing them earlier.

There was now no way they could carry on as William Hill's auditors and they were replaced by Deloitte and Touche. Bizarrely, and partly because of Brent Walker's developing financial problems, KPMG were allowed to remain as auditors for the Brent Walker Group, a decision to which Bob and I strenuously objected and treated with derision. Although they were our parent company's auditors, I refused for a long time to allow anyone from KPMG to walk through the front door of any William Hill office, on the grounds that they were not be trusted. To this day, I have never knowingly given KPMG any work.

Several years later, Allen and Overy, our lawyers, invited me to a management conference on Business Ethics and Integrity. The main speaker was from KPMG. I refused to attend, telling them that there was nothing anyone could learn from KPMG on those subjects, particularly since I wasn't sure they knew what the word integrity meant.

The right and proper thing would have been for KPMG to have said, from the very start, that there was a potential conflict of interest that Chinese walls might not avoid and therefore they couldn't act both for William Hill and Grand Met. It seems that fees or ambition stood in the way of professional integrity. Since then, partly as the result of cases such as Enron and World.com, people are less surprised when accountants behave badly.

As a footnote, the young man who, acting under orders, led the team who carried out the infamous deed resigned from KPMG. He had been such a good contributor to our work that Bob decided to employ him ourselves and he played an important role in our subsequent victory.

After KPMG withdrew as the purchaser's accountants, we were advised by both Deloitte and Touche, and Leigh Carr. Their support was tremendous throughout. For long periods there were up to 25 of their staff working at our offices. The thing that slowed matters down was that the accounting records for 1989 were a complete shambles. For example, it required many man years of effort to sort out the bank reconciliation records and rent records for all our betting shops as well as for the head office.

KPMG continued to play a major part, as Grand Met's accountants, and it was in that capacity that, eventually, they had to be given access to our premises again, something we found extremely distasteful. Their large team spent several weeks examining the original records and they were entitled to talk to our staff and move around the building. Whenever they did, we insisted that they were chaperoned. It was an uncomfortable time for both sides and no doubt unfair to individual KPMG staff members but it was difficult for us not to treat the firm with the contempt we felt it deserved.

Among the various arguments put forward to the expert adjudicator by Grand Met was the argument they had previously put to us: that the principles of acquisition accounting should apply. We disagreed. The expert, Ray Hinton, had been appointed on the basis that he was not required to give reasons for his decision, so he was not going to say which principles he was going to adopt.

Perhaps for that reason, Grand Met suddenly decided to try to obtain a court ruling that the original sale and purchase agreement contained errors that should be rectified. It was a potentially massive complication that threatened to add years to the resolution of the dispute and create enormous additional work and costs. The only consolation was that it suggested that Grand Met's confidence was waning.

Our legal advice was that rectification was very difficult to obtain through the courts, with a high burden of proof required. Two of the top law firms in London had been paid huge sums for their work on the sale and purchase agreement, which had gone through many drafts, taken up hundreds of hours of senior management time and, in its final form, been subjected to minute scrutiny by both parties and their advisors. Now, Grand Met were alleging that the agreement contained a serious mistake. It had not stated that it was the intention of both parties that the business's accounts, divided into the two parts of William Hill and Mecca, should then be combined under the principles of acquisition accounting.

The implication was that it was only by applying those principles that Grand Met could sustain the profit prediction that had underpinned the sale of William Hill to Brent Walker for the agreed price. Grand Met were clearly in trouble. If acquisition accounting was so important, why hadn't they and their advisors ensured that the agreement was clear on the subject? Why couldn't Grand Met produce documents to show that the subject had been discussed and agreed with Brent Walker? Why, given its importance, had the matter not been raised as a major point in negotiations?

There were other questions. Since William Hill had not bought Mecca and Mecca had not bought William Hill, why was acquisition accounting relevant to the William Hill/Mecca business? Under all accounting rules you could not apply acquisition accounting except at the level of Grand Met, the parent company that had bought and then sold William Hill and Mecca, and it was certain that the parties had not agreed to prepare completion accounts at the Grand Met level.

The court case lasted five weeks. All the legal advice we had received came to nothing when Mrs Justice Mary Arden ruled in favour of rectification, apparently because George Walker had said "Right", during the course of one of Sir Allen Shepherd's self-admittedly lengthy monologues. The questions posed above were never satisfactorily answered or dealt with in her judgement.

We were advised to appeal but, in the end, decided against it. It would have meant a further delay and additional costs for an uncertain outcome. We had already spent six years and £30million, all of which would be lost if we failed to win the claim. Our fate was in the hands of Ray Hinton, the expert, now working on the basis of a sale and purchase agreement amended in accordance with Grand Met's wishes. Even on that basis, we remained confident. Let nobody say that William Hill doesn't take or make big bets.

After a final round of oral submissions, Hinton promised a decision for 10.00am on Monday 30 September 1996. Two days earlier, Frankie Dettori's 'Magnificent Seven' at Ascot had relieved William Hill of £8million. Hinton produced a better result for us. He ruled that the correct profit figure for 1989 was just below £46million, almost £12 million less than Grand Met had claimed, and way below the important trigger figure of £51million. For every £1million less than £55million, £12.8million was to be deducted from the purchase price of £685million. The precise figures produced a deduction figure of almost £118million.

Hinton's decision was more than a victory for William Hill; it was vindication. Many people believed that the claim was a smokescreen to hide Brent Walker's financial problems but we had pursued it because we knew that it was a sound claim. Year after year, Grand Met and KPMG had defended the indefensible. It seemed to us that they were playing a long game, hoping that either Brent Walker, its financial ability to continue the struggle, or our resolve would collapse. They didn't.

I had been so confident that we would win that, unknown to Bob and his team, I had booked a jazz band to appear at our office, along with champagne, balloons and streamers, and pinned a superman outfit to the door of Bob's office. For six years, Bob had worked relentlessly on the claim, normally starting work between 6.00am and 7.00am and rarely stopping before ten at night. During the whole period, he took only seven days off, four due to flu, and never took a holiday. The claim work was on top of his normal duties, including work on a refinancing of William Hill and preparations for a Stock Market flotation. Not superman as much as superhuman.

I waited for the telephone call. When it came, the result was total victory. I announced the result over the tannoy at the office and staff set to work decorating the reception area and Bob's office. The jazz band arrived and started practising 'Congratulations' and 'We're In The Money'. At that moment, with balloons hanging from the ceiling and champagne in buckets of ice, a television crew walked through the door with a reporter to interview Graham Sharp, our media officer, about the disastrous loss we had suffered on the Saturday at Ascot. We must have looked like wonderfully good losers. As Bob and his team made their way down the street, back to the office, the band struck up and we cheered them all the way to the entrance. After all we had been through, it was a very moving moment for all of us.

As an afterthought, we phoned Green's Restaurant in Duke Street, one of my and Bob's favourites, and booked their private din-ing room for an impromptu celebration that night for the 20-strong team who had done most of the work on the claim. The restaurant did us proud. So proud that none of us could remember much about it the next day.

*

While we were dealing with the claim, I started to get the business sorted out and make sense of the chaos. At that time, I'd never been in charge of a company before. I'd been part of the management team at

William Hill but this was the first time I'd actually been in charge. It was obvious that the high gearing and high interest rates meant that, unless we achieved healthy profits, we would have serious difficulty in making the interest payments due to the banks. The telephone betting division was in reasonable shape, with Grand Met having centralised the racing systems of the merged businesses in Leeds. New computers were in place but there were problems with the software, which it would take two years to resolve.

The betting-shop division was not so good. The management structure was top heavy and the important area of shop development had been handed to line management, with the specialist team side-lined. The shops were short of staff and some were being closed as a result. No coordinated pay structure for shop managers or staff had been implemented and there was a plague of problems caused by shortcomings at central administration, which meant that bills weren't being paid promptly.

Grand Met had commissioned a report from Inbucon to help them decide on the best location for their administration offices. Was it at Mecca's offices in Wood Green, North London, or at William Hill's in Leeds? Inbucon came down firmly in favour of Leeds. Grand Met ignored their report and moved everything to Wood Green. Staff at the offices in Leeds were made redundant before replacement staff were recruited for London, including the whole of William Hill's wages department, with the result that queried wages became the rule rather than the exception.

My strategy had been outlined in the prospectus we had prepared for the banks. I now set about implementing it. The management board would consist of the senior person in each area of the business: telephone betting, shops, finance, personnel, property, development, IT and marketing. It seems obvious but not all of these areas had been represented before. During my years with William Hill, I had developed very clear views about what needed to be done to run a successful bookmaking company. Now that I was in charge, I intended to put them into effect.

First, management of costs was vitally important. It was one of the few things we could actually control and the quickest way to make more money in any business is to stop wasting it. Secondly, a streamlined management structure was necessary, one in which everyone did their own job and didn't interfere with others. Thirdly, we required a strong shop development team that would extend or relocate 5 per cent of the shops each year, supported by a cost-conscious property department, capable of shopfitting all the developed shops, plus another 5 per cent, making 10 per cent in total. Over a ten-year cycle, every shop would be newly fitted. Fourth, marketing should be price-led and very focused. Fifth, the personnel department should be very commercial and business-focused and under no circumstances introduce a formal appraisal system, something I consider to be the biggest waste of management time ever introduced in any company.

Before we could implement anything we had to appoint suitable people to the relevant posts and restructure the line management and most departments, so that they had fewer people but were more focused. During the first year after Brent Walker had taken over William Hill, a whole new management team was put in place. The operations director for betting shops was Liam McGuigan, promoted from regional director; the telephone betting director was David Lowrey, another internal promotion, along with Bryan Robinson as property director; the personnel director was Steve Olive, returning from the USA after starting his career at Ford; David Hart from Ladbrokes became our development director, with Bill Haygarth, formerly a consultant with KPMG, as IT director. Bill Wilson and Kevin Hogan both rejoined Hills, Bill as Raceline's director and Kevin as company secretary.

It was no time for dithering. We knew that the profits predicted by Grand Met were not going to materialise and unless we acted quickly and decisively we might soon find ourselves in breach of bank covenants for failing to honour our financial commitments, which would lead to all sorts of problems.

I needed people prepared to work hard to manage costs and deliver results while simultaneously streamlining the business. Within the first year we replaced three of the five regional directors and promoted one of the others. We cut the number of area managers by a third.

David Hart got his development team established and development activity under way. It was there that profits could be improved, over time, by extending, relocating and refitting shops, closing down shops that were losing money and getting licences for new ones. Over the next ten years, in over 700 locations, representing virtually half of William Hill's estate, we either re-sited or extended shops, or obtained new licences, while closing loss-making shops. Ninety per cent of the most profitable 200 shops are now to be found among those developments.

From an appearance point of view, Hills' shops were in a mess, with a variety of blues and whites, some red and brown, and some not shopfitted for more than 20 years. Some of the shops bought from Playboy decades earlier had still not had anything done to their interiors. The former Mecca shops were also in an unsatisfactory state but mainly in red and green. When Grand Met took over, they started by changing every Mecca fascia to William Hill, in green and white. I couldn't understand it. For 50 years, William Hill's brand colours had been blue and white, as had their fascia signs when they started owning betting shops. Changing the colours to green and white was like Cadbury changing the wrappers on their Dairy Milk bars from the purple they had always been to green.

Anyway, I don't like green so when, all those years earlier, I was sent to the department run by George Cortesi, who wouldn't allow green, he needn't have worried. There was no danger of me wearing it. Maybe it runs in the family. My gran wouldn't have green in the house. She said it was unlucky. I won't even have a dinner service with green leaves on it. I know it's irrational. Anyhow, William Hill is synonymous with blue and white. That's the brand; why change it?

They had also been changing the interior shop colours to grey and pink. I've never been sure why. I stopped all the pending shopfittings and, together with Bryan Robinson, agreed a design brief with mainly blue and white colours. He set about finding a shop design that was attractive, cost effective, hard wearing and practical. We didn't want wooden writing shelves, because punters write on them; and I didn't want padded seats, because punters are always sticking pens into them and you end up with seats full of holes. I wanted some carpet, so the shops looked luxurious, but not too much, because people put their cigarettes out on the floor.

I wanted seats with their own ashtrays and cup holders, bright lights over the newspapers on the walls and over the counter but lights that wouldn't reflect on the television screens; a good sound system, and the cheapest fire-resistant ceiling tiles available. I've yet to spot a customer looking up and admiring the ceiling. We also adopted Mecca's idea of 12 screens for the display of text, with a very large screen in the centre to show the live racing.

Working with a company called Saunders, Bryan came back to me with a revolutionary concept in betting-shop design. It was brilliant. There was a metal framework against the walls, from which tin wall panels, shelves and betting slip dispensers were all hung. Newspapers were held up by magnetic strips and, if a tin panel was damaged, you simply unhooked it and replaced it with a new one. The whole thing was thousands of pounds cheaper per shop than its predecessors. It meant that we could fit out three shops for the same amount that two had cost William Hill previously and they looked fantastic.

On top of all that, the fittings were expected to last ten years or more, compared with six or seven for existing fittings. That move is still saving William Hill thousands of pounds today because the fittings have, in fact, lasted more than ten years.

We carried out these changes firstly at our shop in Camden High Street and then completed another five. We spent a lot of time visiting the shops and getting feedback about their performance before rolling the design out to the whole estate. If the design was wrong in some way, now was the time to find out, not after we had already done 100 shops. We were on our way with a ten-year plan that would transform the look of William Hill's business on the High Street.

With all my experience as a shop manager, I knew how easy it was unwittingly to create maintenance problems through faulty shop design. For instance, due to a lack of consistency in planning, we found that there were 45 different types of controls for working the central heating systems in our shops, and 57 different time-switch controls for the fascia lights. We adopted one standard control for the central heating systems and one for the time switches.

I'd drive down a High Street at 10.00pm and see a fascia light, switched off. I'd drive down there again at 10.00am and the light was on. Why? Often, it was because new managers or relief managers didn't know where the clock was and couldn't work it even if they found it. During the winter, unless the manager turned the heating off before he went home on Saturday evening, the heating would probably be on all day Sunday, in 1500 closed shops.

We fitted special light-sensitive time clocks so that the lights came on automatically when it was dark and turned themselves off at 11.00pm. We fitted time clocks with Sunday cut-outs for the heating system and made it the responsibility of technical staff, who came to change the camera films, to check the settings of both clocks, thus allowing the manager to get on with running his shop. It took us eight years to get every fascia sign in the country the same and all the clocks standardised but we did it.

The design, the attention to detail and the systematic development of the estate since 1990 has given William Hill the best, most modern shops in the industry, with a turnover and profit per shop higher than any other major chain. It was not achieved by instant, magic wand management, nor creative accounting, but pure hard work, attention to detail and a long grind.

The most important factor in the success or otherwise of a shop is location. Of course, the manager and staff are important but a good, genuine, hard-working manager can only get the business that the shop's location allows him to get. If a good manager is running a shop with turnover of £10,000 a week, there is no way on earth that a slightly better manager will get that up to £15,000. On the other hand, a bad manager can lose business. The fact is that, in 1990, three-quarters of betting shop customers spent fewer than 10 minutes in the shop. They were using it as they'd use a newsagent's on the way to work; for convenience.

When they walked through the door what they wanted most was to be able to look at the *Racing Post* or *The Sporting Life* on the walls, get hold of a pen and a betting slip and have their bet taken quickly. Things have changed slightly since then – people now spend more time in a shop – but location and convenience are still the key factors, followed by service and facilities.

Another focus of attention was marketing. Abstract, waffle-type marketing was not for me. I had a view that, in bookmaking, that type of marketing wasn't effective. It's impossible to create a punter cost-effectively. I wasn't sure how people got into punting but I wasn't going to spend money trying to find out. I liken it to trying to get someone who is teetotal to start drinking. It might be possible but achieving it isn't going to be cost effective for a brewery. What I did know was that the vast majority of those who bet went to the shop that was most convenient for them or, if they bet by telephone, phoned the company that usually answered the phone quickest and which took their bet most slickly. For them, that was the equivalent of the most convenient shop.

The only way to overcome the lure of convenience was by offering competitive prices on more events than anyone else, which is what we did, day in and day out. I would check the advertisements and teletext each day to make sure that no one was betting on something we were not betting on and that our prices were competitive.

What we needed to do was to get Hills' prices into newspapers. Our theme was price-led advertising and, even now, you will rarely see a William Hill advert that doesn't have prices in it; and prominently. For betting shops: location, location, location. For telephone betting: speed, speed, speed. For both, competitive prices on the maximum number of events. Simple but, as events have proved, highly successful.

I remember Corals running a national advert on the Grand

National. It featured former champion jump jockey John Francome. He thinks so and so will win the National, what do you think? And there were no prices. When you wake up and want to have a bet on the National, do you really want to know what John Francome thinks will win, to the exclusion of prices? I don't think so. Most people like to pick their own fancy and then want to know what price it is. You have to think like a punter. It's not hard. I am a punter and I think like a punter. What I want is quick, slick service and to know the price.

When we took over from Grand Met, the head of marketing was following an advertising policy based on puns and cartoons. There were prices on a little strip down the side and a lot of white space. I said, "I'm not paying £34 a square column centimetre for white space." He said, "But it looks really good and the punters love it." I asked him, "Well, if it's so good, how come Hill's telephone business is three times bigger than Mecca's?"

He was also hooked on brand marketing and had plans to spend a lot of money promoting the William Hill brand on large billboards and buses, none of it involving a display of our prices. I told him that we didn't have the money for it and, anyway, it would be a waste of money. We had a well-known brand name; it didn't need building up. What we wanted was other people's customers. If we got them to bet with us just once, and got it right, a fair few would stay with us. As far as adverts were concerned, it was to be prices, prices and more prices, with occasional free gift or free bet promotions.

I did try to recruit a couple of marketing people but they said that, given how I thought, it was not a marketing manager I wanted to recruit but an advertising manager and that's who I finally decided to look for. I promoted David Hickling, who had been at William Hill for a number of years and, from the day I appointed him, I never had to worry about marketing or advertising again. He was rock-solid, hard-working, got in early, left late, checked everything scrupulously. I could rely on him completely. He'd show me the adverts for the big days in good time and I would rarely have any comment to make.

No fancy stuff, no brilliant jokes, but prices and promotions. There aren't generally great differences in prices, because the market drives you towards the same prices as the other big bookmakers are offering but, even though we couldn't offer the best price on everything, we would always be the best price on something, and always in the paper so that customers with other bookmakers could see it. We gave away free binoculars and free umbrellas and then took the plunge and made the phone calls free. I was far from convinced that it would work because I couldn't believe that anyone would choose to change their bookmaker simply for the sake of a free phone call. How wrong I was.

For a long time after we'd launched the free phone service, Ladbrokes were telling City analysts that we were throwing our money away. We didn't say anything because a key part of our marketing strategy was silence. This is a business where your competitors can replicate what you are doing, virtually instantly. If they don't realise something is doing well they won't react. We didn't boast about Raceline and we didn't boast about all the accounts our free phone service was producing. If we had done, our advantage would not have lasted long. If my memory serves me correctly, it took Ladbrokes well over a year to introduce their own free phone service.

About a year before Grand Met bought Hills, we had moved the credit operation to Leeds and introduced a computerised bet capture system that enabled the telephonists to take a single bet in 19 seconds. If you can deal with a customer in 19 seconds, you can start dealing with the next one in 20 seconds.

We'd already got an automatic call distribution system which prioritised calls according to the number they phoned, with higher-staking clients given one number, middle-ranking customers another and a third number for smaller punters. When they made a call, they all came to the same switchboard but the priority numbers went to the front of the queue, if there was one. This had increased turnover considerably and ensured that our bigger customers always got first-class service. If you treat everyone the same, you end up taking a £5 bet and missing out on a £200 bet.

After a few years we were looking to upgrade that equipment when BT approached us to try a new system. It replaced our in-house call distribution system with a much more sophisticated BT-based one. It could tell us how many people were waiting, how long they were waiting, and how many calls we were losing on the off of races. It prompted us to train most of the administrative staff to take telephone bets so that, close to the start of a big televised race, or when we saw a build-up of calls, we could suddenly have another 50 people taking bets. It was the idea I had seen in operation in the USA a few years earlier.

In 1991, we briefly and exclusively launched credit card betting – an initiative from David Lowrey, our telephone betting director. On the first day we did it, Grand National day, we advertised in every national paper and set up special phone rooms to cope with the expected demand. The phones were ringing before 8.00am, every spare body was manning them and you couldn't put a phone down without it immediately ringing again. They were still ringing after the field had jumped three fences. BT complained that the sheer volume of attempted calls had blocked their network in some areas.

On the Monday there were complaints in the press about allowing people to run up debts on their credit cards and within two days the banks had stopped it but it had shown us the potential. Once again, the importance of convenience when betting had been demonstrated. What could be more convenient than picking up the phone, giving a card number and placing a bet? For many customers, particularly occasional bettors, it was preferable to going down to the betting shop and avoided the hassle of applying for a credit account weeks in advance of its intended use. True convenience in telephone betting had arrived and had promptly been banned.

Later that year, I noticed that Switch cards, which were debit, not credit, cards, were being introduced. So we approached the banks to propose using debit cards. The answer was a tentative yes but every transaction over £10 would have to be cleared manually. I couldn't see how that could work. It would be too slow and cumbersome, not a convenient way of betting at all. David Lowrey disagreed. He thought the banks wouldn't be able to cope with all the manually cleared transactions and would quickly relent. So we went ahead and he was proved right. The banks couldn't cope and within months the transactions were fully online. We were the first of the major bookmakers to introduce debit card betting and could take a bet from a first-time customer in one minute and their subsequent bets in 20 seconds. It was a tremendous success; one of our best-ever innovations. By 1995 debit card betting accounted for over one third of all Hill's telephone betting turnover and by 1998 it was up to 47 per cent.

The ultimate proof that our approach to marketing worked came that year, when the Monopolies and Mergers Commission looked at the merger of Ladbrokes and Coral. They found that, in 1997, by turnover, Hills had 42 per cent of the telephone betting market with Ladbrokes, our nearest competitor, having 26 per cent. That particular market is the absolute test of marketing in the bookmaking industry because a telephone betting business is not capital intensive and can be set up quickly and cheaply.

The Tote was always claiming that it had the biggest telephone betting operation in the world but we just smiled and kept quiet. We knew we were miles in front and it pained us when, because of the MMC, our figures were revealed. We wanted to keep it to ourselves.

Having reduced other annual costs by about £1 million through the management restructuring, we then looked at operating costs and how they might be managed more effectively. I'd always thought that money was being wasted and one of the first things I did was insist that no one was to travel by first-class train. Ninety-nine per cent of train travel by William Hill staff was between London and Leeds, a journey time of only two hours. It just wasn't necessary to go first class. There were a few exceptions, such as if a woman was travelling in the evening on her own and felt intimidated but neither Bob Lambert nor myself had one first-class train ticket in the next ten years. Staff like to see the boss travelling second class and it saved

£50,000 a year, at that time equivalent to the annual profit from one middle-grade betting shop. We also introduced an 'all diesel' car policy, because diesel was cheaper and in London everyone was told to use public transport rather than taxis.

We formed a small committee called 'Cut the Crap', which went into the minute detail of expenses. The sort of proposals it came up with were that all mail must be sent second class unless it was urgent and very few pieces of mail were urgent. The company was using big, A4 envelopes so that A4-sized paper didn't have to be folded, but those envelopes were three times as expensive as the smaller ones, so we switched to the smaller ones.

We kept chipping away at our suppliers' prices and even got rid of the rented potted plants at our head office. Bill Warren, the *Racing Post*'s advertising manager, told me he knew we and he were in trouble when, on a visit to discuss increasing the price of advertisements, he saw the plants being carried out of the building. By then, because of the recession and Brent Walker's problems, we were in trouble – and he never got the price he wanted for the advertisements.

CHAPTER SIX
DOUBLE TROUBLE

George Walker had bought businesses with big, unsecured loans and, when he sold a business, or part of a business, he didn't use the money to repay the loans. He used it for working capital. In the early 1990s the long boom finally ran out of steam, the recession set in, the asset value of Brent Walker's business fell, and Brent Walker found itself short of cash and in trouble. It was owed a considerable sum by Grand Met but it would be six more years before that was proved and the money paid.

Bookmaking businesses generate a lot of cash and, right from the start, Brent Walker's treasury department were on the phone to borrow money from us. They weren't just taking our money out of the bank, they were using our overdraft facility as well. Frankly, I hadn't appreciated the implications but Bob Lambert was very unhappy about it. He went to see Brent Walker's finance director, Wilfred Aquilina, and told him he didn't think they could take the money. Aquilina not only insisted that they could but that there was documentation to prove it. This statement was supported by John Hemingway, a former partner in a leading law firm and a non-executive director at Brent Walker. Wilfred went further. He said that the banks were aware of it, Brent Walker had put £285million into William Hill themselves and therefore were entitled to use the cash flow and overdraft facilities for group purposes.

Bob told Aquilina that he was going to charge Brent Walker interest on the borrowed money and at a higher rate if it forced Hills to use their overdraft facility. He insisted that Hills would have to have the money back when it was needed, in particular to enable monthly betting duty payments to be made to Customs and Excise, and to pay the interest on our loans. As time went on, the more our cash built up and the more Brent Walker took. Eventually, their borrowings reached £45million. There was little cash in William Hill's bank account and our overdraft was fully drawn. When we told Brent Walker that we needed £11million back to pay Customs and Excise, we were told we'd have it by 11.00am the next day, which was payment day. It didn't come. It had been held up.

"As a matter of interest," one of Brent Walker's directors asked, "what happens if Customs and Excise don't get their money?" Bob told him, "Then, at their discretion, they can demand next year's estimated payments in full, up front, charge interest, and possibly have our licence taken away." We still didn't get our money until the last minute, and then only half of the £11million, followed a few days later by the other half.

We were becoming very uncomfortable with the whole business. It was becoming clear to us that Brent Walker had real cash-flow problems. Bob was then asked to sit in on a meeting between Aquilina and John Ross of Hill Samuel, who were lenders to both Brent Walker and William Hill. Among other questions, Ross asked for confirmation that Brent Walker were not using Hill's money to support their own cash flow. Wilfred evaded the question and gave a non-committal answer that Ross appeared to accept. Immediately after the meeting, Bob told Wilfred that, unless he explained the true position to the banks within 24 hours, he would tell them himself. Wilfred told them the next day and all hell broke loose.

Bob and I came in for heavy criticism from the William Hill Group's banks. When they found out that Brent Walker had Hills' money, Bob and I got a nasty letter from Slaughter and May, the solicitors acting for the syndicate of banks who had lent money to William Hill, telling us that we had no right lending the money and that they were considering whether or not we were personally liable for any losses that resulted. We fought them off with some difficulty. Fortunately, the fact that we had charged Brent Walker interest and that our accounts made no attempt to hide the situation counted in our favour. Brent Walker continued to argue that they had the right to borrow from William Hill and obtained legal advice that said that, at worst, the position was unclear.

Bob and I were right in the middle, between Brent Walker, our parent company and employer, and William Hill's banks. I said to Bob, "I'm going to be the shortest-lived chief executive that William Hill has ever had. Either Brent Walker will get rid of me, or the banks will."

Eventually, after a lot of pressure from the William Hill banks, Brent Walker somehow managed to repay most of the money and we got the balance when, some time later, Brent Walker was refinanced. In the meantime, a new agreement was put into place which clearly outlawed loans from William Hill to Brent Walker. But not before Brent Walker had asked us for more money, which we refused. I then got a call directly from George Walker, which was rare. He wanted me to transfer £5million or £10million; I don't remember the exact figure. I told him that the banks had made it clear that we couldn't do it. He became very angry. "I bought that business. It's my money. If I say I want £10million sent over, you send it over." I said, "I can't do it, George." We were put under tremendous pressure but we didn't send it.

*

By November 1990, less than a year after Brent Walker had bought William Hill, the shares had tumbled, and Brent Walker were trying to get shareholders to agree a £103million bond issue, with George

Walker putting up £27million himself. A standstill on loan repayments had also been agreed with the banks until the end of 1991 and a £1billion refinancing deal was being discussed. Since Brent Walker couldn't meet its banking obligations, its future, and William Hill's, was entirely at the disposal of the banks.

At about this time, George called a meeting of the trustees of the William Hill pension scheme. There was a surplus in the pension fund, which Brent Walker had paid for as part of the purchase price paid to Grand Met. The purpose of the meeting was to approve an investment in Brent Walker. This was clearly an important matter but there was neither time nor sufficient information available to take professional advice in advance of the meeting.

There were seven trustees, four from William Hill and three from Brent Walker. We had recently told pension scheme members that the pension fund would be kept totally separate from William Hill and Brent Walker, and all four William Hill trustees decided to oppose the investment. I was on holiday in Lanzarote and gave my proxy vote to Bob. John Hemingway, one of the Brent Walker trustees, was also absent and gave his proxy to Tim Quinlan.

George chaired the meeting and recommended that £2million be invested in a Cayman Island company which would then invest a larger sum in the Brent Walker bond. Bob explained the William Hill trustees' concerns, there was a discussion, and a vote was taken. Remember, this was before the scandal involving Robert Maxwell who, after his death in November 1991, was found to have raided his companies' pension funds in order to support his companies.

George and Quinlan voted in favour of the proposal but Keith Dibble, Brent Walker's company secretary, very bravely voted against. The William Hill trustees joined him and Bob didn't exercise my proxy because my vote wasn't needed and he thought it better to keep my relationship with George intact.

Immediately after the meeting Bob and I agreed that the proposal might be made again and that the trustees should be fully prepared. We obtained advice from Titmuss Sainer & Webb, and from Counsel, accepting responsibility for the cost ourselves. Two days after the first meeting, a second meeting was called, with no agenda available.

Before the meeting took place, an article appeared in the London *Evening Standard*, explaining in detail what had occurred. It must have been leaked to put pressure on Brent Walker not to proceed. I didn't approve of the leak and neither Bob nor I were responsible for it. Brent Walker were justifiably furious and attention switched from the investment proposal to the leak. However, it may have served a purpose because the meeting was abandoned and, at a later meeting, the fees which Bob and I incurred were accepted as a proper responsibility of the pension scheme.

George was clearly unhappy. For several months he didn't talk to me. Eventually I spoke to Sam Burns and told him that things couldn't carry on like this. Either the issue was dead and buried or we had to resolve it. Through Sam, I invited George to Sandown to present the trophy for the William Hill Hurdle. He accepted and at Sandown behaved as if nothing had happened. We were on good terms again.

George's proposal was mentioned once more – more than ten years later. George visited me at William Hill's office to discuss his business in Russia in relation to SIS, of which I was a director. As George left, he bumped into Bob. "Hello, Bob," he said, "I thought you'd retired." Bob replied, "I have but I stayed on as chairman of the pension trustees for a year." George said, "I couldn't think of a better man for that." With mutual best wishes, Bob went on his way. George turned to me. "Thank God he never let William Hill put that money into the Cayman Islands," said George.

At the end of 1990, at the insistence of the banks, Wilfred Aquilina was forced to step down as finance director of Brent Walker, to be replaced by John Leach, who later became chief executive. In January 1991, George Walker was replaced as chairman by Lord Kindersley, formerly deputy chairman of Lazard, although George continued as chief executive, for the time being. Just prior to that, George had asked me to join the Brent Walker board, so I became a director of a Stock Exchange-listed company. It seemed a good thing at the time. I didn't know that George was opposed to Lord Kindersley's appointment.

At his first board meeting, Kindersley talked about the collapse in the share price and told us that his task was to build value for shareholders. Then George said he wasn't going to put up with interference. If Kindersley had plans to do this or that, so be it, but George made it clear that he was running the business. It was a difficult meeting. There was clear antagonism and it became very uncomfortable.

The previous March, William Hill had submitted its claim against Grand Met, in relation to their over-statement of Hill's 1989 profits. In September 1990, Brent Walker refused to pay the deferred £50million to the William Hill Group, who therefore were unable to pay it to Grand Met, who took legal action against William Hill for non-payment of the £50million.

At first, the banks showed no interest at all in our claim. Like everyone else, they assumed that the claim and Brent Walker's refusal to pay the £50million was a case of "can't pay, won't pay". The more they realised the seriousness of Brent Walker's problems, which meant the seriousness of their own problems, the more interested they became in the claim.

With the resignation of KPMG, Brent Walker appointed Touche Ross to advise us, partly because their chairman, Michael Blackburn, was a racing and betting enthusiast. Later, he would become a non-executive director of William Hill, a good friend, and my partner in Shooting Light. We gave Touche Ross's representative an overview of the situation and I told him that I didn't think the claim would take long to resolve. I was wrong. In February 1991, a court ruled that the William Hill Group had to pay the £50million outstanding on the purchase price. We couldn't and didn't pay, and the legal action rumbled on for years, with Grand Met, at critical moments, threatening to seek a winding up order against the William Hill Group.

They never went through with the threat, for good reason. If they had, William Hill's operating companies would have been sold and, with the William Hill Group heavily in debt to the banks and to Brent

Walker, Grand Met would probably have ended up with only a very small part of the £50million.

In September 1990, Brent Walker claimed that their profits during the first half of that year were up over 50 per cent on the first half of 1989 but the following May they delayed the publication of their results for the whole of 1990 and warned that there would be huge writedowns in their assets. When the accounts were finally produced, they were heavily qualified by the auditors, who stated that the profits previously announced for the first half of 1990 had been materially overstated. In fact, instead of a profit, there was a pre-tax loss of £256million and a £600million writedown. It was getting very messy and the banks started to press for George Walker's resignation as chief executive. George was never going to resign.

To add to the uncertainty, someone at Stanley Leisure, one of the biggest betting and gaming companies, kept suggesting they'd done a deal with George and were buying two casinos and a couple of hundred of Hill's shops. It was in the newspapers quite regularly, it was undermining the business and staff morale, and it was getting on my nerves. Eventually, I phoned Stanleys and told them that if these stories didn't stop, I'd ring the *Racing Post* and tell them that Hills had made a bid for Stanleys. We were in negotiations to buy them. I'd be bidding £1 but I wouldn't tell the newspaper that. The stories stopped.

At the end of May 1991, Hugo Kindersley phoned me to say that a board meeting was being arranged at which it would be proposed that George be removed as chief executive. If we didn't remove him, the banks were going to put Brent Walker into liquidation the next day, which they could do, because Brent Walker had breached its bank covenants. Kindersley asked which way I'd vote. I told him that I would listen to what was said at the meeting and make up my mind but if the situation was as he had described it, and the banks were committed to that course of action, it would heavily influence my decision. I asked him if the company's lawyers would be there. He replied that it hadn't been arranged. I told him I considered it imperative because the whole board would need the best possible legal advice before coming to a decision of such magnitude. In my heart I knew that it couldn't be right to jeopardise Brent Walker's and William Hill's futures by allowing Brent Walker to be put into receivership. I believed it would be the duty of every director to take the actions necessary to avoid it.

Behind the scenes, there were huge rows. Banks who had lent money to Brent Walker wanted to use Hill's profits to shore up Brent Walker. Banks who had lent money to Hills, but not to Brent Walker, including major institutions such as Deutsche Bank, the Bank of Nova Scotia and the Industrial Bank of Japan, weren't too concerned about Brent Walker, unless it collapsed and brought William Hill down with it. Some banks, like Standard Chartered and Lloyds, had lent large amounts of money to both Brent Walker and Hills.

Because of Grand Met's legal action against William Hill, and the judgement that the £50million was payable, Hills was in breach of its bank covenants and technically could be asked for the repayment of its bank loans, although that was in no one's interests. With an unpaid debt of £50million, our claim against Grand Met outstanding and the recession biting into profits, William Hill would fetch nowhere near the £685million Brent Walker had paid for it.

It was a very difficult time. I remember one major meeting chaired by Eric Nasland, a senior executive with Standard Chartered, responsible for debt recovery. The directors of Brent Walker and William Hill were there, along with their lawyers; the banks were there, with their lawyers; even the potential administrator was there, in case Brent Walker went into receivership. There were more than 50 people at the meeting, with double rows of chairs around the table, and professional fees totalling tens of thousands of pounds an hour being clocked up.

Nasland wasn't a typical banking executive. He was a rough, tough East Ender. He started by making a long statement about the position of the banks in relation to Brent Walker, and insolvency. When he noticed that Nicholas Ward, Brent Walker's chief executive, was taking notes, he challenged him. "What are you doing?" Ward responded, "I am writing down what you are saying." Nasland told Ward that he hadn't come to have him write down what he was saying and walked out to a stunned silence. The only sound was that of the lawyers working out their bills.

Eventually, Brent Walker's and William Hill's banks agreed that the William Hill Group would be more strongly ring-fenced from Brent Walker than it already was. The board would be reconstructed with three members, including the chairman, from Brent Walker; Bob and myself from William Hill; and two independent directors, Michael Blackburn, who had recently retired from Touche Ross, and Graham Elliott, formerly a director with Slough Estates. It meant that neither Brent Walker's executives, nor William Hill's, could control the board without the support of the independent directors.

More importantly, the loan agreement with the banks was strengthened. No money could go to Brent Walker, either as a loan or to pay interest or dividends, until the £50million payment to Grand Met had been settled and William Hill were up to date with their capital repayments. A rock-solid ring fence now surrounded William Hill. These changes, despite our parlous financial state, involved paying a fee of, I think, £8million to the bank syndicate. Breaching bank covenants is a very expensive business.

Settling the claim would have helped, and Brent Walker, encouraged by their banks, tried to negotiate a settlement with Grand Met. But it wasn't Brent Walker's claim, it was William Hill's, and any money that was recovered would be due to William Hill and their banks, not Brent Walker. Bob and I took legal advice and were advised that Brent Walker could not settle the claim independently of William Hill. In a bizarre episode, Lord Kindersley, in his capacity as chairman of Hills, was obliged to write a letter to himself, as chairman of Brent Walker, spelling out the situation to himself!

With the crucial board meeting about George Walker's future coming up and affairs reaching a climax, I arranged for some 'Business As Usual' advertisements to be prepared and called a private meeting of senior racing journalists at Green's restaurant in Duke Street. There was the possibility that Brent Walker would be put into receivership and, although the William Hill Group was ring-fenced and its operating companies financially sound, who could tell what the impact on our business would be? Scare stories in the press could be very damaging. I assured the journalists that the William Hill business was sound and ring-fenced from Brent Walker and asked for their support in reporting the situation correctly. To a man they promised they would do everything they could to help.

We had prepared a television advertisement to convey the message that Brent Walker's situation would have no effect on the William Hill trading businesses and that at William Hill it would be business as usual. The advertisement would show a jockey in racing silks gradually entering the picture from the bottom of the screen, with our explanation of the situation above him, until finally the whole jockey was on the screen, with the message, "Now you've got the full picture." Fortunately, we didn't need to run the advertisement, but it was a close-run thing.

On the day of the board meeting, I went up to Brent Walker's offices at the Trocadero near Piccadilly Circus at about 6.00pm and George took us all for a meal at a Brent Walker casino in Park Lane. We talked about everything other than the board meeting. At about 8.30pm, we went back to the head office and the board meeting began. Lord Kindersley explained the situation. If we didn't remove George as chief executive, that night, the company would be put into receivership. George said the banks were bluffing. We shouldn't allow them to bully and bluff us.

At one point Malcolm Williamson, the chief executive director of Standard Chartered Bank, came in and addressed the board on behalf of the syndicate of banks. He said that they were only willing to continue to support Brent Walker and restructure the loans if the board removed George, who insisted vociferously that the banks were bluffing. Williamson, who is now president and chief executive of Visa International, said that not only was he not bluffing but he would put it in writing. He went out and came back with the ultimatum, in writing, no ifs or buts. It didn't seem to me that they were bluffing.

Williamson left the boardroom and Kindersley then asked Alan Carr, the senior partner at Simmons and Simmons, to advise the board. Carr said that he could not believe that the head of Standard Chartered, which was the lead bank for the syndicate, would put such an ultimatum in writing if he did not intend to carry it out. The board should assume that the bank syndicate did intend to put Brent Walker into receivership if it failed to remove George and, under those circumstances, it was the clear fiduciary duty of the directors to vote for George's removal. As distasteful and unpalatable as it was, it seemed there was no choice. It was the directors' duty to act in the best interests of the company's shareholders and, if the board took action that ultimately led to Brent Walker being put into receivership, the directors may well be personally liable for any loss suffered by the creditors and shareholders.

There followed an impassioned address by George, who criticised the banks for 30 minutes. He regarded Brent Walker as his company. He pointed out that, during the previous year, he had put £27 million of his own money into the company, which he had, and that Michael Smurfit and 'Tiny' Rowland had also put in substantial sums, as personal friends of his. They had but the money had quickly gone.

There were 15 on the board, which was very large and included several people who were long-time associates and employees of George. One director hadn't turned up. His train had conveniently broken down. It was getting very late, after midnight. The bank team were waiting for our decision. Eventually, the chairman called for a vote, by a show of hands.

I voted against George. It was the worst moment of my business life. I was voting to remove the man who had put me in charge of William Hill and put me on the board of a public company. I considered myself a friend of his but I couldn't let my liking of George stand in the way of preventing Brent Walker being brought down. As unpalatable as it was, I didn't have any doubt about which way to vote. It seemed to me there wasn't a choice.

When Lord Kindersley asked those in favour of George's removal to vote, John Brackenbury put his hand on the side of his face. Brackenbury had been chief executive of G & W Walker, the forerunner of Brent Walker, for which he ran a chain of pubs, later to become Pubmaster. "John, are you voting or have you got your finger stuck up your nose?" asked Kindersley. It was the only time I ever heard Hugo Kindersley be anything other than proper. It showed how emotionally charged the meeting was. "No, I am not voting," said John, "I'm abstaining."

The vote was six in favour of George's removal, five against, and three abstentions. I felt ill and angry. Some of the people who voted for George to stay were long-standing personal friends and, of course, included his wife. They would still have voted for him even if you'd told them that they'd be shot if they did. It was the directors who had abstained whose decision I couldn't understand and about whom I felt very angry.

Brackenbury was in the same position as me. He knew his duty. Another one was John Lewis, a senior partner in Jaques and Lewis, a firm of solicitors, who I believe was a personal friend of George Walker's but, of all people, should have known his duty. I didn't want to vote, either, but we had all heard the company lawyer tell us what our duty was, as directors, and I thought their behaviour was irresponsible. Both Brackenbury and Lewis later said that, if George had won, they would have called for another vote and voted against him!

At the next meeting of the directors, I lashed out at them. Kindersley said he could see no useful purpose in discussing the way individual directors had voted but I insisted. I said they shouldn't remain on the board and Lewis did eventually resign. George himself, and his wife Jean, were still on the board as non-executive directors, and he and his family still owned 27 per cent of Brent Walker's increasingly worthless shares, but he was no longer chief executive.

George wasn't one to give up. Less than a month later, he launched an action for wrongful dismissal and breach of contract, claiming £22million. A shareholders' meeting was held at the Café Royal to agree an increase in Brent Walker's borrowing powers. George handed out letters to the shareholders, denying that the banks had made his removal a condition of a £1.4billion restructuring, and calling for their support. Lord Kindersley insisted that George's removal was a condition demanded by the banks.

The two of them kept clashing, there was a barrage of questions from the floor and, when another meeting was held at the Café Royal a few days later, on 2 July, in an attempt to remove George and Jean Walker, and John Hemingway, from the board altogether, things got even worse.

Kindersley didn't get through his opening remarks before George interrupted him. When Kindersley asked Hemingway, a non-executive director, if he would like to say a few words Hemingway stood up, said he wasn't really prepared, then delivered a 30-minute eulogy to George and slated everyone else. It was a brilliant off-the-cuff speech and, at the end of it, the vote went George's way. They were still on the board and Brent Walker still owed the banks about £1.4billion. The shares valued Brent Walker at only £17.5million. We didn't know if they'd sell William Hill or float us or what would happen or when.

The vote didn't alter the fact that George Walker was no longer chief executive. Later that month, Ken Scobie took his place. The board then met monthly, with just the chairman, Scobie, and George and Jean Walker meeting at the offices of Simmons and Simmons, with everyone else, other than George and Jean Walker, meeting as a committee to run the business.

*

At the end of August 1991, when the refinancing plan was still being negotiated, Lord Kindersley called in the Serious Fraud Office after an internal review revealed irregularities. The police took away a lot of documents, mainly to do with Brent Walker's film and property interests. Just before Christmas, George Walker and his wife finally resigned from the board. We just got on with running the William Hill business.

The *Daily Mail* ran an article suggesting that Brent Walker was again teetering on the brink of disaster and that William Hill would be affected. It wasn't a malicious article but it could have been damaging. Channel 4 were showing racing that afternoon so I phoned John McCririck and asked if he would broadcast a statement from Hills in response to the article. With producer Andrew Franklin's agreement, John presented the article and our response, which nipped any problems in the bud, something for which I have always been grateful. Who knows what might have happened otherwise.

In March 1992, what was by then a £1.6billion refinancing was completed and, a few months later, after an argument with the banks, Lord Kindersley stood down as chairman and Ken Scobie stepped in as temporary acting chairman, both of Brent Walker and William Hill. He wanted to be appointed permanently but in the end the banks forced him out as well.

Lord Kindersley, Scobie, and Nicholas Ward, the group's managing director, had all worked long and hard on the refinancing and the banks had apparently agreed to pay various people a bonus. Bob Lambert and myself were each to get £75,000 and Scobie, Ward and Kindersley were to get a lot more. Seventy-five thousand pounds wasn't to be sneezed at. I got the cheque and paid it into my bank. The next day, Bob rang. "Is that money in your bank?" I said, "Yes, I paid it in yesterday." He said, "So did I. Bad news: they've stopped the cheque." And they had.

Standard Chartered Bank claimed they had not approved the payments and that the sums were too big, and stopped all the payments – except Scobie's. For some reason his cheque had cleared, and he refused to give the money back. Later, they decided that my payment, and Bob's, could go through. I don't know what happened about the others but the episode may have been a factor in Scobie's removal. John Leach, Brent Walker's finance director, told me that Scobie would be going but Ken hadn't been told.

That wasn't right. He was a good man, much too nice a guy to be treated like that, and he had been there through all the turmoils we'd experienced over the previous year or two, so I volunteered to speak to him, phoned him in his office and told him I needed to see him. When I saw Ken, I told him that the banks no longer wanted him in the business and that he was about to be out of a job. He got his lawyers on to it. The company gave him a decent package and he went. So Brent Walker, and William Hill, were looking for a new chairman and the queue of applicants wasn't very long. In fact, there wasn't a queue at all. If you have been on the board of an insolvent company, you have to declare it. It doesn't look very good on your c.v. and Brent Walker were certain to go into receivership or administration at some time in the future.

The situation had its bizarre aspects. Brent Walker were technically insolvent, a situation which posed real dangers for the directors. One wrong step and their personal assets could be on the line. At each board meeting, the company's lawyers, Simmons and Simmons, were present to advise the board on the legal correctness of any decision. Eventually, they advised the board that they were owed so much money by Brent Walker that their advice might be deemed not to be impartial. The board couldn't pay them because to do so would have been giving them preference over other creditors, which they advised us was unlawful in a potential insolvency situation. We had to employ another legal firm to advise us and pay them on a meeting by meeting basis.

The story doing the rounds was that Malcolm Williamson, of Standard Chartered, happened to be sitting next to Sir Keith Bright at a function and mentioned that they were looking for a chairman for Brent Walker. Bright didn't realise that he wasn't the first person to be asked but was the only one to say yes.

Anyway, in January 1993, Sir Keith Bright, formerly head of London Transport, was appointed chairman. When he arrived, he gave us the line about being a team player. As soon as the leader of a company says that, you know you're in trouble. So it was early 1993, Bright had just arrived, George Walker had been arrested by the fraud squad, charged with conspiring to falsify company accounts, and declared bankrupt. Nicholas Ward had resigned as Brent Walker's managing director and, by the summer, Brent Walker had breached its banking covenants – again – and still owed £1.4billion. In the first half of 1993, Brent Walker had made an operating profit of £27million but had then had to pay interest charges of £98million.

The banks that had lent £350million to William Hill, led by Lloyds and Standard Chartered, were due to get their money back by 1 March 1994 and the William Hill board were advised by Hill Samuel that we should not assume that they would cave in and roll the loan over for a further period as the deadline approached; in fact, the non-Brent Walker banks were telling us that there was no hope of the loan being extended. We were making about £50million profit a year but were only able to pay the interest on the loan, not make any capital repayments.

The banks who had lent to Brent Walker weren't prepared to take on another £350million loan to a Brent Walker subsidiary, so the only way of repaying the debt was to either sell William Hill or float it on the Stock Exchange. We were advised by our bank syndicate and lawyers to go for a float.

Floating is onerous. It's time-consuming and expensive; involving legal advisers, corporate advisers, marketing advisers. Preparations for a flotation cost several million pounds and the banks weren't united in wanting a float. In fact, behind the scenes, Standard Chartered and Lloyds, who were big lenders to both Brent Walker and William Hill, were telling Bright, who was chairman of both Brent Walker and William Hill, that William Hill was not to be floated but that they wouldn't put up the money to buy out the other banks either.

So Bright sat there as chairman of Hills, saying that he agreed with the flotation, which it was his fiduciary duty to do, while it seemed to us that, behind the scenes, he was doing everything he could to delay and obstruct it. We got as far as the prospectus being printed and approved. Then Lazard, who were acting for Brent

Walker, gave a presentation to the Brent Walker banks at which they argued that, if Hills was floated for £500million, which was the likely value in 1993, they'd be losing out and they'd be better off refinancing William Hill.

The trouble was, Lazard assumed that the National Lottery, which was announced that autumn for launch in 1994, wouldn't seriously affect the business, and that a flotation might jeopardise our claim against Grand Met, which still hadn't been settled. I told them that the claim wouldn't be affected and that it was a high-risk strategy to act on the basis that the Lottery wouldn't affect us.

A few weeks later, just as we were about to send out the prospectus, something that happens towards the end of the whole process, we got a call from Lloyds and Standard Chartered to say that they wanted to see the board of William Hill and the board of Brent Walker, at Lloyds' offices, immediately. They told us that the two banks were going to guarantee, in writing, to repay all Hills' other banks their money. So we had the choice of continuing with the flotation or being refinanced.

Our lawyers advised us we had no real choice. There was always a risk with a flotation, whereas the banks had offered the certainty of refinancing. Just before Christmas 1993, we pulled the float. The theory was that, in a couple of years' time, as the economy came out of the recession, Hills would be worth more and Hills was the glue that held Brent Walker together while it built up and sold its other assets, notably Pubmaster. For Brent Walker's bankers and shareholders, William Hill and its claim against Grand Met was the hope factor.

The year in which we pulled the float, we made over £50million profit. Two years later, with the National Lottery having been launched in November 1994, we made only £40million so, in the short term, their theory didn't work out too well. By then, we were worth less than the new bank syndicate had lent us. Their loan was under water and they were sweating but William Hill was still their only hope of salvaging something from the wreckage. So it was decided that it would be a good idea to incentivise Hills' management. Two schemes were suggested: an annual and an exit scheme.

In 1993, we'd made a profit of about £55million but had had to pay interest of about £35million, so the net profit was £20million. The annual scheme, which Bob and I insisted should cover everyone down to area manager level, was based on beating the budget figure for net profit. If we got it up 25 per cent, to £25million, we got 50 per cent of our salary as a bonus. A 25 per cent increase in the net profit was only £5million. I told them it was a scheme that was against their interests, and that the scheme ought to be based on pre-interest figures but that's what they wanted. "We're in here," I told the management team. "In like we've never been in before."

By the end of the year, the National Lottery was affecting us badly. It was obvious that we had no hope of reaching £50million profit before interest payments and, after a six-month review period, the budget figure was set at £39million – representing a post-interest target of just £4million. When we actually made £40million, that extra £1million represented a 25 per cent increase on the budgeted post-interest profit of £4million, so we got 50 per cent of our salaries as a bonus. On the other hand, if profits had fallen even slightly short of £39million, the bonus would have been wiped out completely.

The banks were not pleased but I told them it was not my scheme, it was their scheme, and produced the letter I'd written to Lazard telling them it was inappropriate to base it on post-interest profits. Meanwhile, in June 1994, George Walker and Wilfred Aquilina, Brent Walker's former finance director, appeared in court on various false accounting, theft and conspiracy charges. In October, George was cleared while Aquilina was convicted on one charge of false accounting. When George emerged, he immediately had another go at the banks.

*

George Walker had regularly been on at me to get William Hill into the USA, where Ladbrokes were operating. He kept suggesting that we buy this racetrack and that racetrack, and wanted us to take a look at all of them. I didn't want to go and couldn't spare the time and Len Cowburn, who had stayed on as deputy chairman, didn't want to go either, so when Ian Spearing applied for a job after being made redundant by Ladbrokes, I took him on and sent him.

Every time George suggested a track, we put Ian on a plane, he'd spend a few days investigating, then come back and usually tell us it wouldn't work. In any case, because of my experience in Belgium, I've always been very opposed to getting involved with betting shops overseas. I can't think of any venture that has been very successful. You are trying to sell a gambling product in a market you don't know, which is highly regulated and where you need government support, which you're not going to get.

Eventually, George got his way but not until he'd left Brent Walker. After he'd been cleared of fraud, he set up a company called Premier Telesports and started to beam British racing into betting shops in Russia and the Eastern Bloc. He obtained the licence to run the Moscow City Lottery and lived in a dacha at Moscow's Golf and Country Club. Later, he sold the lottery licence for several million dollars.

In 2003, Walker sued the Racecourse Association and Attheraces for allegedly breaching the contract which gave him exclusive rights in Eastern Europe. The court case revealed that the operation had not been a financial success and, after Walker, by then aged 74, had endured a gruelling cross-examination, his barrister asked for an adjournment to consider the position. The next day, a settlement was announced that left George facing heavy legal bills and Premier Telesports' licence was terminated.

CHAPTER SEVEN
LEADING FROM THE FRONT

Len Cowburn only stayed on for a few years after Brent Walker's takeover of William Hill. He concentrated on his work as a member of various industry bodies, including the Levy Board, the Betting Office Licensees' Association and the Bookmakers' Afternoon Greyhound Service. During that time, Len was invaluable to us. With all the trouble we had inherited and the problems associated with Brent Walker, I would never have been able to cope if industry affairs had been stuffed into my already bulging briefcase. It was an especially difficult time for me, personally, because in 1993, after a long illness, Jenny died from cancer.

Although I let Len do his own thing, he found it a difficult situation and eventually decided it would be best to retire and enjoy the rest of his life without the strains of big business, something I always felt I would do too when the time came.

After Len left, I started to get involved in the political side of things for the first time. The Home Affairs Committee had looked into the horserace levy system in 1991 and Len, who was then chairman of the Bookmakers' Committee, had given evidence. Later that year, the Marquess of Hartington, who was senior steward of the Jockey Club, announced plans to set up the British Horseracing Board. By the time it was launched, in 1993, with 'Stoker' Hartington as chairman, the government had already agreed to some deregulation and tax changes. In 1992, betting duty had been cut from 8 per cent to 7.75 per cent, with the savings going to racing, and in 1993 betting shops were allowed to open in the evenings, from 1 April to 31 August.

As usual, the racing industry wanted bookmakers to pay more, and 'Stoker' Hartington organised a series of private meetings involving senior members of the BHB and leaders of the betting industry. I thought 'Stoker' was very good. He chaired the meetings well and he wanted to understand the bookmakers' position and the economics of our business before forming his views. I regarded those meetings as a great success. Of course, we didn't agree on everything but each of us came away with a better understanding of each other's position and at least we were talking and listening. How that was to change after 'Stoker' stood down! I am sure those meetings played a major part in our reaching a five-year levy settlement in 1994 – the longest ever – at a time when the National Lottery was looming.

Tristram Ricketts, who had been chief executive at the Levy Board, became the BHB's chief executive. He's now their secretary-general. Tristram was an ideal recruit for the job. At the time, the need was for discussion and consensus to bring together the vested-interest groups that made up the BHB's board. Tristram was well suited to that. He is someone I like very much and admire for his administrative skills but Tristram should never have been given the title 'chief executive'. His job was really that of general secretary and he did it well. How, in any case, can you have a board but not have the organisation's chief executive sitting on it? That was the situation at the BHB.

Tristram has a particular skill, an administrative skill. He under-stands the industry and he's invaluable to other people but he's not a dynamic leader and when he's been criticised for that, I've always thought it was unfair. It's criticising him for not being what he was never going to be. It's not his strength and it's not what he was recruited for. It takes all sorts to make an organisation work and you can't have everyone on a white horse, saying, 'Charge!' Tristram was good at making things happen behind the scenes, at getting papers ready and presentations made, and he does an awful lot that no one ever sees. There are not many people I come across of whom I'd say, "That man can work for me" but Tristram is definitely one of them. If he'd been available to work for a bookmakers' trade association, he would have had my full support.

Not that we've been in dire need of him. At the Betting Office Licensees' Association, and now at the Association of British Bookmakers, Tom Kelly has played that role exceptionally well. Tom, who was the editor of the *Sporting Chronicle* until its closure, has been one of the main advantages the betting industry has had over the racing industry in their debates during recent years.

Tom makes sure that the betting industry's view is put over properly, articulately, and consistently. Rather like William Hill in Brent Walker, he is the glue that has held us together. It hasn't always been easy for him at BOLA, where he has had to sit in the middle when the big bookmakers have argued with each other, and with the smaller bookmakers, and ensure that business is dealt with in an impartial way. I have nothing but admiration for Tom. I am sure that, without his efforts, the bookmaking industry would not be as well off as it is today. His well-crafted papers at the time of the move offshore by Victor Chandler, then Ladbrokes and Hills, were a significant factor in ultimately securing a gross profits tax. He and Warwick Bartlett were the architects of the ABB, which includes just about all the bookmakers' trade associations except the National Association of Bookmakers.

The National Lottery was my main concern at the time the BHB was set up. The first draw was on 19 November 1994 and Hill's operating profits for the first half of 1995 were £22million compared with £33million during the corresponding period in 1994. That gives you an idea of how hard the Lottery hit us. You can imagine the mood among the banks, especially as they had just refinanced us rather than let us float. Once again, we would be in breach of our bank covenants and perhaps unable to make capital repayments.

It was obvious that the Lottery was having a devastating effect on our business and on racing's income through the levy. I mentioned it to John McCririck, who suggested that I appear on Channel 4 Racing's programme from York to talk about it, which I did. I called for a cut in betting tax to help the industry compete with the Lottery. Frankly, I was very nervous. I wasn't used to appearing on live broadcasts and came across like a wooden top but at least I got the message across. The industry picked it up and lobbied hard. All our staff and those of other bookmakers wrote personal letters to their MPs about the unfair competition from the Lottery.

It worked. That November, Kenneth Clarke, as Chancellor of the Exchequer, announced a 1 per cent cut in the rate of betting duty, from 7.75 per cent to 6.75 per cent, which enabled us to cut punters' deductions from 10 per cent to 9 per cent. We had tilted at a windmill and knocked it over – but it wasn't enough.

For some inexplicable reason I have always been able to analyse problems and find innovative solutions. I also have the knack of recognising good ideas from the management team, or knowing which idea just needs a bit of development to make it work. Contrary to some people's opinions, William Hill was not a one-man band. We had a talented, hard-working and creative team and not all of Hills' ideas were mine – I only wish they were. For example, introducing a free phone service and credit cards weren't my ideas, although introducing debit cards was. Some of my best ideas or analyses of problems have occurred to me while on the regular, long drive down the M1 from Leeds to London. I used that time to turn a problem over and over in my mind until a way forward emerged.

One day in 1995 I was driving along the motorway, thinking about the National Lottery, and what we could do. When it was introduced, it had been made illegal for bookmakers to take bets on which numbers would be drawn in the Lottery. At William Hill, we produced a paper for submission to the government, arguing that we should be allowed to do so. It was a well presented, well argued, logical case and, in my view, one of the best that William Hill ever produced. We circulated it to all the relevant figures in government and to dozens of MPs but to no avail. We still can't bet on the National Lottery. In 2001, the Budd Committee recommended that bookmakers be allowed to but the government, by then a Labour government, rejected the recommendation. This was a government that constantly espoused the virtues of competition but it didn't seem to want any competition for its own product, a position almost certainly in contravention of European Community law.

Still, I always believed in tilting at windmills. You don't win all the time, in fact you lose more than you win but there is no disgrace in losing, only in not trying. Fear of losing or of rejection should not stop anyone from trying. If it does, very little will ever be accomplished. We had tilted and failed. What were we to do? We knew that Irish bookmakers were betting on the UK Lottery. In fact, at that time quite a chunk of their entire turnover was in bets on the UK Lottery. I thought, there's nothing to stop us betting on the Irish Lottery and perhaps that will embarrass the British government into letting us bet on the UK Lottery.

If we were to cause maximum embarrassment, the best way to do it was through SIS's service into betting shops, as an industry product. So I spoke to Ladbrokes and Corals and, quite quickly, Corals said they didn't want to do it, which immediately killed the notion of an industry initiative through SIS. I've never really understood why they weren't keen but, like Ladbrokes, they had shops in Ireland and perhaps thought it would upset the Irish government. We carried on talking to Ladbrokes, to Chris Bell and Alan Ross, who initially seemed keen but at the last moment also decided against it. They didn't think it would make any money, which to me missed the point entirely. "Sod it," I thought. "We'll do it ourselves."

So we dropped the idea of doing it through SIS and worked out that it would only cost us about £10,000 to launch the bet in every William Hill shop. David Hickling picked the name 'Lucky Choice'; we produced a poster, provided each shop with 100 special betting slips, and a bit of chat about it over our audio system. Punters had to choose from one to five numbers to come up in the Irish Lottery draw, which took place twice a week. We offered fixed odds against getting either three, four or five numbers correct.

It was a low-key launch on a shoestring budget and, when I got the turnover figures for the first week, in November 1995, exactly a year after the UK Lottery started, I couldn't believe how good they were, although one punter had managed to pick five correct numbers for £1, at 99,999 to 1, which was a little worrying. However, within about three months, Lucky Choice was making us £150,000 profit a week, equal to almost £8million a year; all for an initial outlay of £10,000.

Why did we do it and not Corals or Ladbrokes? All I can say is that we were always trying new things, without being fearful of being wrong. We accepted that we would make mistakes and were prepared to either live with them, or change as we went along, which isn't a culture prevalent in many organisations.

Adopting our usual stance, we kept very quiet about our success. We didn't tell anyone in the industry and particularly not Corals or Ladbrokes. When they asked how it was going we just said, "All right. It helps to put pressure on the government to let us bet on the UK Lottery." In fact, as far as we could tell it was having no impact in that direction at all.

About six months after its launch, I got a call from an area manager in Bristol to say that John Morgan, who was Coral's managing director, had been into one of our shops and asked how Lucky Choice was getting on. We knew then that he had worked it out and, soon afterwards, Corals started to bet on the Irish Lottery. Several weeks after that, Ladbrokes, the self-styled market leaders, joined in.

Given the success of Lucky Choice, which only took place twice a week, I quickly began to think of other ways of developing numbers betting. A few years earlier, I had spent five days in Las Vegas on holiday and had come across a numbers game called Keno. It operated with 80 numbers: you picked up to 15 numbers and got paid out depending on how many of them came up. At every bar in the casino there were pencils for you to fill in a Keno card; in the coffee shops, every table had Keno on it; there were Keno girls walking around to take your entry and bring any winnings back to your table. They even had a Keno text screen on the television in your hotel room and you could phone up, choose your numbers and see the draw on the screen. The cost was added to your room bill.

I got excited about it and when I got home I sat down with Ian Spearing and said, "Let's get the law books out. We've got to do this." We eventually decided we couldn't but, once we'd launched Lucky Choice, I started to think about it again. If the Irish Lottery had a machine putting balls into a drum, why couldn't SIS do the same, and do it four times a day? We went back to Kevin de Haan, the barrister who had advised us that we could bet on the Irish Lottery, and asked for his opinion on the legality of taking bets on a draw run by SIS. His advice was that it would be fixed odds betting, not a lottery, and therefore legal.

In the draw we had in mind, if everyone backed the winning numbers they'd all get paid out at the same odds, unlike a lottery, where the more winners there are, the less each of them wins. For it to be credible, punters had to see the draw as it happened, so it had to be shown on SIS, and had to be an industry initiative. By then, Ladbrokes and Corals appreciated the value of numbers betting. We arranged a meeting and told them about the idea and showed them the legal advice we had been given. We proposed setting up a joint-venture company and this time they didn't need any persuading. Together, we set up 49s, a name chosen by Chris Bell, because that's how many numbers there were.

We then approached other bookmakers to try to get their agreement to the draws being shown on SIS and proposed that 49s Limited be non-profit making. It would cost each shop only £5 a week to cover SIS's charges and marketing. The National Association of Bookmakers objected to paying the same £5 a shop as the big bookmakers and, in the end, we stopped talking to them, went to SIS and bought two time slots, five minutes in the morning before racing started and five minutes just after it finished.

We launched in December 1996. The bookmakers who chose not to sign up didn't receive the two five-minute transmissions but, when 49s quickly became a major success, most of them changed their minds. Within a couple of months, 90 per cent of SIS's customers had signed up and, at that point, SIS made 49s part of their package and draws started to take place during racing, as well as before and after it. That year, Hills' turnover on numbers betting was about £19million and in 1997 it was more than £52million, about 3 per cent of our total turnover but a far bigger percentage of our profits.

In 1998, we launched another numbers game: Magic Numbers. Customers picked four numbers out of 20 drawn, with a new game every 10 minutes. We were first with that, too. We were fighting back against the impact of the National Lottery, and restoring the profits we had lost, and all because William Hill had had the courage to launch Irish Lottery-betting on a national scale.

Eventually, in 1997, Camelot took 49s to court, claiming that we were running a lottery. Feeling nervous, I appeared in the witness box at Bow Street Magistrates Court, with Chris Bell and Bob Scott, from Ladbrokes and Corals, looking on. Cross-examined, I agreed with Camelot's barrister that the draw looked like a lottery draw, with numbered balls spinning round a drum, but there were vital differences. It was a sterile event, with no one taking part in it. If someone had a bet with us on the Miss World contest, I said, it didn't mean they were taking part in it. In the same way, if someone had a bet on the result of a 49s draw, it didn't mean they were taking part in that, either.

And if everyone backed the same numbers, and they came up, they would all get paid at the same, fixed odds, unlike a lottery. Kevin de Haan, who is now a QC, was vindicated in the advice he gave us. The magistrate, Ronald Bartle, ruled that, "The predominant aspects of 49s are of betting and not of a lottery." He ordered Camelot to pay our costs.

There was also progress on other fronts. When betting shops were allowed to open in the evenings for the first time, in 1993, there was a lot of talk about the problems involved in opening shops at night but I was a great believer in evening racing. What was needed was a 'can do' mentality. Organisations have a great propensity for inventing problems. You have to ask what you can do, not what you can't do.

Managers within William Hill were saying that female staff wouldn't be able to get home safely in the evenings and we'd have to get taxis for them. Managers were spending hours agonising over how to deal with it. My approach was: let's not invent a problem. There were plenty of other High Street businesses, such as fast-food shops, where staff worked in the evenings. If a problem arose, we'd sort it out. Until then, we should just get on and do it.

We took a very positive attitude and opened a lot more shops in the first year of evening opening than other major bookmakers and we got a lot of business as a result. We had identified the fact that people who had a bet in the evening would often have to go back to that shop the next day to collect any winnings and, because it was convenient, would probably place their next bet there. It wasn't just about making a profit from evening racing, it was about convenience, continuity and keeping your customers and it showed in our results.

*

William Hill had shown how to respond to competition: by innovation. The National Lottery was a big blow, and had unfair advantages over us but we fought back by using our imagination and developing new products and by lobbying the government to carry out more deregulation and reduce the tax burden. What the BHB did, in 1996, was replace 'Stoker' Hartington with Lord Wakeham, who already had a long list of jobs. Although he was no longer Leader of the House of Lords, Wakeham was chairman of the Press Complaints Commission and the non-executive director of several companies, including the Enron Corporation, which would cause problems for him several years later.

I couldn't really see why the BHB took him on. Wakeham had a reputation as a political 'fixer' who would bring some sort of political influence to bear but you wondered how much that could help racing. Also, he seemed to be one of those people who looked for consensus in everything. That approach might work in politics but in commercial organisations someone has to take the lead and make decisions. Consensus means that you never get the best of anything, you never take the best decision, you always accept less than the best. How can you make progress when you are always settling for less than the best? It is one of the problems that the BHB have not yet overcome – if it can be overcome with their board and voting structure.

All organisations have to have leadership and the team leader, whether he's chairman or chief executive, has to make decisions. When I was chief executive, chairing William Hill's operating board, I regarded it as my job, and everyone's job, to put their point of view forcibly and listen to what others had to say in order that we all fully understood the matter before us. The more vigorous the debate, the better we all understood the subject and the more likely it was that we would reach the same view about the right way forward. But – and it is a big but – the right decision was not a voting matter. If, as chief executive, I was not convinced that the general view was the right view, it was my job to take the decision, not the committee's job. The chief executive is paid to get it right. He stands or falls on getting it right. At William Hill, we didn't take decisions based on consensus or majority votes.

For example, if it was suggested that we join Tote Direct and everyone except me was in favour of joining, we still wouldn't join unless I was persuaded that it was the right decision. I didn't go to committee meetings to count votes and I didn't go to reach a consensus. I went to hear what other people had to say, so that I fully understood, listened to their arguments and formulated my view. If it was completely different to everyone else's, I would think very carefully before proceeding but, having thought some more, if I wasn't persuaded by the majority view I would take a lone decision. This didn't happen very often but it happened. For example, I was the only one at William Hill who wanted to launch betting on the Irish Lottery after both Corals and Ladbrokes had pulled out. I insisted, against the views of the majority.

Consensus isn't leadership and neither is having a vote and saying, "Right, the vote's six to five in favour, so that's what we'll do." You don't need a chairman to do that; a secretary can do that. My attitude is that you are getting paid to run a business and any silly sod can be chief executive of a business where all the important decisions are taken by a majority vote. You could never be fired because you could always say, "No, I counted the votes correctly. It was definitely six to five; I wrote it down." That doesn't work. In my view the chief executive should make the decisions and if he makes wrong decisions, he goes. That's what business is all about.

People think that I'm autocratic but I'm not. My style may be difficult to live with because I always put my views strongly, supported by sound reason and logic. I expect my top team to stand up and do the same. I insisted on a very open environment at William Hill, with no secrets and no politicking. I always take difficult decisions. I never fudge them. If anyone asks what I think, I tell them, even if I know it's not what they want to hear. I'm hard and I have firm views but my leadership style isn't autocratic. Autocracy is when you impose your will without listening to anybody. You have to listen, and the arguments have to be hammered out over the table. Then, and only then, are you in a position to make a decision.

We have had fierce debates, even out-and-out rows, at team meetings. We have shouted and violently disagreed with each other. Bob Lambert and I have had incredible rows but that is my style because I need to have a testing argument in order to reach a clear view on an issue. I keep pushing and pushing. I know I give the impression of being stubborn, pig-headed and absolutely refusing to move. I will sit and argue until the cows come home but the next day I will do something different because I've assimilated the arguments and reached a different view. So the exercise has worked. I've got out of it what I wanted: a better-informed decision.

I have a reputation for being tough but I believe that I should also have a reputation for doing things correctly. This type of management style requires a strong-willed top team and I was fortunate in having one. It was not unusual, after a particularly difficult meeting, for one or more of the team to come back to me afterwards and say, "You are definitely wrong and this is why." We would then revisit the subject again and often the decision was changed.

Richard Evans, *The Daily Telegraph's* racing correspondent, calls me a dinosaur. He sees me as a defender of the past but, if you look at William Hill's record, we are the ones who have led the industry and changed everything. Free phones, credit and debit card betting, numbers betting and, later, Gross Profits Tax. I think of all the changes William Hill have proposed or introduced yet I've got this reputation for living in the past. I've never understood it.

Maybe it's because, when I've done my analysis and argued about it, I know exactly where I am and what I want to do and I can't see any point in negotiating about it. I'm an open book; a totally open book. If I'm intimidating, it's because I've done my homework. I hold strong views and I'm willing to express them strongly and back them up with facts but they're not views I've come to lightly.

Len Cowburn once said I had ice in my veins. I think he meant that I was cold, that I didn't consider if I was upsetting people, and I suppose I don't. I don't notice. In my view, that's both a strength and a weakness. I also don't notice or worry about what people think of me. I see my job as to do the right thing for William Hill, first, second, and third, whatever reputation it gives me. When I was sitting with Len Cowburn, my boss, in front of Sears, and was asked what I thought of moving the business to Leeds, I said what I thought, that it was wrong, and I paid the price. I got sent to Belgium for three years but at least I didn't sit there and pretend to agree with Len, so as not to upset him, when I didn't agree with him.

That's what I encouraged the top team at Hills to do and they did. No one in my team ever got sacked for saying what they thought or for trying things and getting them wrong. They only got into trouble for not trying things.

If I'm hurting people's feelings I really don't notice but I don't think

I'm cold. It's not that I don't care about people, because I do, but in my view the chief executive's job is to care about the business first and people second. In the long run, people will be best served if they are working in a strong business.

When I first took over at William Hill I was told that people were frightened when they knew I was going to be in charge. Morale was low and what was I going to do about it? I told them, "Nothing, absolutely nothing." We were going to run the business in a certain way and do certain things and, if they turned out right, morale would take care of itself. Even if I'd decided to work on morale, I wouldn't have known how. How do you improve morale except by making a business successful?

I admit I was never over-generous at patting people on the back. I've never looked for it myself and never really saw why people needed it. The top team at William Hill were paid well and were treated more generously than is the norm in similar situations in other companies. In fact they all made several million pounds from their efforts. I have never asked them, "Do you want to be regularly given a pat on the back for doing the job or get well paid?" Despite never having put that question to them, I think I know what their answer would be.

Funnily enough, William Hill himself had a similar reputation to mine. We certainly had a motley crew. I've had people work for me whom I've been told were poor managers of staff. In reality, aren't we all? Who ever met a really good man-manager who also produced great results? I certainly haven't met that universal genius yet.

And it was only the results in which I was ever interested, not how they were achieved or how good a man-manager someone was. David Hart, our development director, had a reputation for being particularly frustrating as a manager of people and frustrating to his colleagues in his management style. The only thing I cared about or noticed was that he and his team produced 60 or 70 good shop developments year in year out, and nobody in his team was leaving, so he must have been doing something right. Every year, for 12 years, we had 60 or 70 shops extended, or re-sited, or got new licences and, at the end of the 12 years, 90 per cent of our 200 most profitable shops came from those developments.

I see people's strengths and ignore their weaknesses. I've only ever seen what people *could* do for William Hill, not what they *couldn't* do. I always concentrated on the results, not how they were obtained. David Hart was delivering exactly what I wanted delivered. How was he doing it? From a man-management point of view, maybe poorly; maybe not. I didn't care: he was doing it, getting the right results, and that's all I cared about. He was executing more developments than anyone else in the industry, winning more court cases over re-sitings and new licences and objections to other bookmakers' applications. That's what I cared about. That was good enough for me. I don't believe in appraisals and I don't believe in sitting down and saying, "You're a poor manager. I'm going to send you on a course to improve your management skills." It's a waste of time. If a tiger's got stripes it's no use sending him along to the cleaners to have his stripes washed off.

It was similar with everyone in the team, including myself: I got results. Another example was the guy running marketing: David Hickling. I had the greatest regard for him. He'd be there at 8.30am every morning and leave at 6.30pm. There wasn't an advert that went into a newspaper that he hadn't scrutinised, letter by letter. He drove advertising agencies mad with his attention to detail and price awareness. Was he dynamic? Was he your typical marketing man, full of charisma, ego and jargon? No, he wasn't. Did that worry me? I couldn't have cared less. All I knew was that the job was getting done, in exemplary fashion. We were opening more accounts per week than any other company and clearly the advertisements were working and he was producing results on a tight budget. We had 40 per cent of the telephone betting market, which is the test of whether your marketing's working, and it was David Hickling who was doing the marketing.

There used to be an advert on television for Home Pride flour with a team of grain graders who all looked exactly the same. You often see management teams like that: everybody looks the same, acts the same and responds the same. I couldn't live with that. I call that style, 'pimple on the nose management'. If you don't conform to the mould, if you've got a pimple on your nose or sport a moustache, you're out. Did David Hickling have a pimple on his nose? I've no idea. I didn't notice.

The Hill's management team had plenty of weaknesses and the equivalent of pimples on their noses but they all had certain things in common. They got results in their own areas, they were resilient and determined, which they had to be, working for me and for William Hill in the circumstances we were often in. As for their weaknesses, I ignored them and, in return, they put up with mine. You can teach people to do certain things but in my opinion you can't change how they are, or their personality, and it's a waste of time trying. Better to build on their strengths and ignore or try to mitigate their weaknesses.

The way we did business at William Hill was different from the way Ladbrokes did business. Ladbrokes were at their best as a bookmaking business when Cyril Stein was in charge. Then, they were the industry leaders and moving forward when Hills didn't seem to be. Stein was managing by making things happen and Hills seemed to me to be just managing, as in getting by.

Then Ladbrokes bought Texas Homecare and got involved in US racetracks and betting shops in Holland and various other things that didn't work and it's never been quite the same since. At one time, before Brent Walker bought Hills, Ladbrokes were reporting results that indicated they were making more money per shop than us but it wasn't clear whether that was really the case. There wasn't sufficient published detail to be sure but it was strongly rumoured that they had one overseas customer who was losing millions of pounds to them, betting over the telephone.

Since 1995, Chris Bell has been in charge. At times, I found him frustrating, and I'm sure he found me frustrating. His approach is one of wanting to be all things to all men and, as a result, I was sometimes not sure what he really thought. He prefers to take a political approach rather than deal with issues head on.

The style at Ladbrokes under his leadership is to meet people behind the scenes to work things out. That is alright unless it is an industry matter, in which case it should be dealt with when everyone is present. The diplomatic approach is fine providing you make your own position clear but diplomacy is often about fudging an issue and I think Chris's approach often does that. When he's across the table from someone, or at a meeting with the BHB, I often can't tell whether he's for something or against it. He may not have said he's for it but he won't have said he's against it, either. That's Chris's style and, it has to be said, it works for him. I can't do that. If I think someone believes I support something when I don't, I tell them there and then that I don't. That said, we all develop a style that suits our own personality and I think our different styles have helped to make our industry associations work well.

At Corals, Peter Sherlock, who later died tragically in a road accident, arrived on the scene in 1991. Corals were owned by Bass and Sherlock, who certainly looked the part and talked the part, came from another part of Bass. When Mike Snapes, Coral's chief executive, left, Sherlock took charge himself.

I remember going to a meeting at the Levy Board with him. Beforehand, it had been agreed that one person would speak for the bookmakers and it wasn't him. We'd hardly sat down before he took over, committing Corals and us to all sorts of things. In the end I couldn't stand it any longer. I had to interrupt him and tell Sir John Sparrow, the Levy Board chairman, that what Sherlock had said did not represent the views of William Hill and I did not either accept or agree with a single word of it. Sherlock may have been a major corporate player at Bass – and he may have been good at that – but he was definitely not my type.

At that time Corals had about 950 shops and Sherlock announced an investment programme to upgrade them. Nothing wrong with that, but he also decided to get rid of the 150 shops with the lowest turnover. In running betting shops, you need to get the benefit of economies of scale. Those 150 shops may have been the worst performers but the vast majority of them wouldn't have been losing money; they would have been contributing to the overheads. At Hills, we only got rid of a shop if it wasn't contributing to the overheads. After Sherlock had left, Corals spent the next few years trying to get the shops back. They bought the Arthur Prince chain, Michael Tabor's business, for a big price, a chain that included some of the shops Sherlock had sold for lower prices.

In 1992, Sherlock set up Tote Direct with Lord Wyatt, the Tote chairman, to put Tote terminals into betting shops. It was senseless. The Tote is a competitor. When I walk into Selfridges, there are several in-store concessions such as Chanel and Christian Dior. Selfridges aren't paying Chanel for them to be there; Chanel are paying Selfridges. With Tote Direct, you had the Tote coming along to Brent Walker, who had paid £685million for William Hill, to ask Hills to pay £4,000 for each Tote terminal, in order to sell their competing product, with Hills providing the space and staff to sell them, in return for commission. It was a one-sided and flawed concept. It wasn't an 'over my dead body' situation but for me to have been interested the economics would have had to make sense. They didn't. If the Tote had come along and said, "We'd like to rent 30 square feet of this shop and put someone in to take bets through a machine we'll supply and pay you a percentage of the bets we take," I would have said, "That sounds interesting; let's discuss it."

At first, Ladbrokes didn't join but later they did. Chris Bell told me that it was for political not commercial reasons. I never understood that: business reasons I could understand but not political ones. At that time, if we'd had a vote at William Hill on whether or not to go into Tote Direct, I would have been nearly alone in opposing it. The easiest thing in any business is to follow the herd. I sweated blood over it. A 'no' was going to bring a lot of criticism and I mulled it over for a week. If we didn't go in, I knew we'd get flak in the press and, if Tote Direct was a massive success, we'd have lost ground and maybe the chance to get shares in the business.

But all the mathematics told me that the right business decision was to stay out and although it seemed a difficult and high-risk decision, it fitted in with a philosophy of mine. You always have to ask yourself whether a decision is one you can reverse and what the costs are.

Although this was certainly a big decision and one that could cost Hills money in the short-term, it wasn't irreversible; it wasn't a one-off opportunity. We might have lost the chance to have shares in Tote Direct but even that wasn't certain. If it turned out that I was wrong to have stayed out, I thought I could always reverse the decision in the future and join. I presented this analysis of the situation to the management team and the board agreed that we would stay out but keep the situation under constant review.

That was a lesson I had knocked into me early at William Hill. No one is always right and when you make a bollocks of something, don't be frightened to backtrack. There's no shame in acknowledging that you've made a mistake. Nobody's a universal genius. You will make decisions that are wrong and then you have to try to get out of them. And you can get out of them more easily if you don't put yourself in a box.

That is the biggest single failing in management – being wedded to an idea and not admitting that it is a failed idea. If it doesn't work: stop it. But many big organisations and management teams are incapable of admitting mistakes and backtracking. At Hills, there is absolutely nothing we have done which we are not prepared to stop doing and change the next day.

That approach also teaches you what decisions should be made by whom. Decisions that can be changed tomorrow can be taken by lower level management but decisions that can't be changed tomorrow and could be expensive, need to be taken by senior management or the board.

One of the criticisms that could be levelled at Peter Savill, who became chairman of the BHB in 1998, is that he seems to find it difficult to admit that a policy might be wrong and backtrack. It may be that he has never worked in a big business at a high level but has always run his own business, I don't really know, but it seems to me that he often takes an entrenched position early on, when he doesn't need to, and insists that he's not going to move from it until he's in a position where he can't move without losing face. That happened, for instance, in 2001, when he was adamant that he wouldn't agree to data charges being based on gross profits; they had to be based on betting turnover. That may have contributed to the failure to agree a levy settlement and meant that the government had to determine the levy that year. Of course, in tune with the switch to a gross-profits-based tax, the government ruled that the levy system should also be based on gross profits.

To some people, Peter and I may look very similar in our approach.

We certainly both believe in analysing problems to arrive at solutions, in trying to change things, and in the chairman or chief executive taking decisions but there are clear differences in approach and implementation. How often have you seen Peter put a letter in the press, or even an advert, attacking his own industry? You haven't seen me do that. I would never publicly criticise my own industry.

It doesn't mean I don't comment in the press. I do and I also encourage our management team to do so. When we were owned by Sears, the philosophy was not to talk to the press. I daren't speak to them and the chief executive wouldn't speak to them. When I took over I told people that, if a journalist rang, they must ring back and that they had to say something. They should make sure that what they said wasn't libelous but apart from that, the only words they weren't allowed to utter were, "No comment." I wanted to establish William Hill as a company that had a view as an industry leader.

If a journalist rings me, I always ring back. I never miss. Even if I'm on holiday in Florida, I'll ring back and try to say something helpful. Racing journalists are a pretty good bunch and not a single journalist has ever let me down. Anyway, Ladbrokes joined Tote Direct in 1997 but it hasn't been a success for anyone. It's a millstone around the Tote's neck. By the time they've paid Corals and Ladbrokes their commission, there's hardly anything left for the Tote.

Peter Sherlock suddenly left Corals and John Morgan came back from Bass for a second spell as managing director, presumably as a safe pair of hands. Later, after he'd retired from Corals, Morgan became chairman of SIS.

Angus Crichton-Miller had recently become chairman of the Racecourse Association and the two men, who knew each other from previous business dealings, got into discussions about the contract between SIS and the RCA covering the sale of pictures to betting shops. In my opinion, Angus, who had been a director at Rank, was running rings round John. Angus was saying that, when the RCA's contract with SIS came up for renewal, three or four years from then, they would look favourably on SIS if they agreed to change various terms of the then current contract. I sat on the SIS board, getting angrier and angrier.

At one meeting, I even called for a vote of no confidence in Morgan, with no hope of winning it, but I just couldn't stand it any longer. I said, "If Crichton-Miller is saying the RCA will look more favourably on SIS in three years' time, why don't you get him to write down exactly how favourably?" I thought it was pretty naive. Crichton-Miller might not even be there when the time came to negotiate a new contract. In fact, when the time came, he wasn't there any more. This was in 1998 and, in July of that year Morgan resigned.

At Corals, Sherlock had sold a lot of shops but I wasn't a great buyer of shops. I never have been, which might seem surprising. I think the only big chain of shops I've ever been involved in buying was the chain belonging to Playboy. I could only ever see the risk in buying at high prices, not the opportunities, and could never bring myself to pay the price.

When you buy shops, you are always in competition with other bookmakers. It's like a horse sale. People start bidding and you make the final, winning bid, and you've bought a yearling for 100,000 guineas. The first thing you think is, "Great, I've got it, and for the price we were prepared to pay." What you should be thinking is, "There are 300 potential bidders here and I'm the only one prepared to pay 100,000 guineas for this horse.' That is a worrying thought.

It's the same with betting shops. When you've bought some for millions of pounds, it means that you were the only bookmaker willing to pay that much. No one else was prepared to pay as much. And that's the way I've always thought. It's probably a weakness. I am not sure I have the real courage needed to be a big buyer but I am a great believer in investing in the business you've already got. Fortunately for me, during most of my time as chief executive at William Hill, we didn't have any money to buy other businesses, so it was academic.

CHAPTER EIGHT
ALL THE WAY FROM JAPAN

It was just as well that, in September 1996, Ray Hinton, the adjudicator in our claim against Grand Met, ruled in our favour because a few months earlier Brent Walker had reduced the book value of William Hill from £696million to £428million. Brent Walker still had debts of about £1.5billion and was talking to its bankers again. When wasn't it?

Brent Walker shares were trading at 3p, which was probably 3p more than they were worth, and there was even the possibility of selling most of our shops to Ladbrokes. The merchant banks suggested that Bob and I could arrange a management buyout of William Hill, on the understanding that, simultaneously, 1000 of our best shops would be sold to Ladbrokes. The theory was that Ladbrokes would be prepared to pay a substantial premium for shops that would immediately raise the quality of their estate and that although William Hill's management would get the remaining 500 shops and the telephone business for relatively little, the exercise would still raise more than any other method of disposing of the business.

We had a series of meetings with Chris Bell and Paul Usher, Ladbrokes' finance director, and they expressed interest but eventually the proposal was rejected. It was, anyway, far from certain that the Brent Walker banks would have agreed to the sale and there would have been competition issues. In November 1996, Brent Walker sold Pubmaster, its chain of pubs, for £171million, which left only William Hill and a few properties. By then, we were beginning to recover from the National Lottery and the banks started to look at the options for selling us. We were getting back towards profits of over £50million a year, and a price of between £500million and £600million was discussed.

Bass, who owned Corals, looked the business over, and there was a bid from a Malaysian leisure and gaming company, but the front runners were venture capitalists, including Electra, Charterhouse, CVC Capital Partners and Cinven, and a consortium of NatWest Ventures, Prudential Ventures and Baring Private Equity Partners. At quite a late stage, Nomura's name popped up. None of us knew much about them in the venture capital field, although we knew that they were a huge international financial services group with headquarters in Tokyo.

If a management team aligns itself with one venture capitalist, then the others tend to drop out because they operate by putting up a certain amount of the purchase price themselves whilst borrowing the rest from a syndicate of banks. The banks aren't going to lend them the money if the management team isn't on their side. So Brent Walker, which now had Sir Brian Goswell as its chairman, worked hard to keep us out of the negotiations. We could only meet with the venture capitalists in the presence of Brent Walker and its advisers, Close Brothers.

When they'd produced a shortlist, including Bass, Electra, a consortium led by NatWest Ventures, CVC and Cinven, and Nomura, we were allowed to discuss their proposed terms with them. The bids from Bass, Electra and NatWest were lower than the other two, while the terms CVC and Nomura offered management were similar.

When we asked Nomura for details of their funding of the acquisition, the arrangement seemed superior. They were going to put up the whole purchase price themselves and then syndicate it afterwards but we were suspicious that they would buy the business and then the funding terms they were quoting for a future syndication would not be deliverable. Also, at that time, they didn't seem to be in any rush to sell the businesses they had bought, whereas we knew that the established venture capitalists would want to sell as soon as it made financial sense to do so. That was their sole purpose in life. As soon as a venture capitalist buys a business, they start thinking about an exit strategy to sell the business for more money.

Nomura's team was exciting. It was led by Guy Hands, who was in his late thirties and was the head of Nomura's private equity operation. Hands already had quite a reputation. When he was with Goldman Sachs, he had made a fortune for some American investors by latching on to the potential of trailer parks in Arizona. After he joined Nomura, in 1995, he bought a chain of 1800 pubs for £250million, sold 900 of them for other uses, and quickly made a profit of £176million. By the time he left Nomura to set up his own operation, his team, the Principal Finance Team, was responsible for a substantial part of Nomura's profits. At one time, he was reputed to have been given a bonus of £35million.

You couldn't help but like him. He was dynamic and most of his team were young and clever. The team leader for Nomura's bid for William Hill was rather older, Doctor Richard Golding, a highly qualified physicist and a total brainbox. He and his young team would analyse a problem to the nth degree but, unlike Guy, would take an age to reach a decision. They loved analysing things. They produced hundreds of charts and possible scenarios.

I liked them, they were very stimulating and we were leaning towards Nomura. Then, near the end, they produced revised details of their banking deal, which had looked so good when we'd discussed it before. It was worse than CVC and Cinven's. I phoned Bob Lambert and said, "We've finally flushed them out. This is going to make the choice easier."

At our team meeting, only one person wanted to go with Nomura, because of the funding concerns. So we phoned CVC and told them that we were going with them. Normally, the other bidders would have dropped out at that stage, knowing that the management had chosen someone else. That weekend, on Sunday 28 September 1997, I went racing at Ascot. On the way, I bought a *Sunday Telegraph*. Slapped across the business section was the headline "Nomura will fire William Hill team". The article claimed, "Nomura has tabled the highest bid but William Hill management, led by John Brown, managing director, has tried to block it by favouring a lower offer from CVC."

It looked as if Nomura was going ahead without our support, having apparently offered £700million compared with the £650million offered by CVC and Cinven. Hands was allegedly going to tough it out, fire me and the rest of the team and put in a new management team, which he was supposed to have ready.

Later, after Nomura had bought the business, Hands asked me who had put the story in the paper. I told him I thought he had but he said he hadn't and that it had caused problems for him at Nomura, who at the time hadn't known that William Hill's management wasn't on board with them. I suspected the story came from someone at CVC or Cinven but it may have been the journalist's creation. Wherever it came from, there was no truth in it.

A few days later, late one evening, Brent Walker held a board meeting to decide to whom to sell Hills. Although I was a Brent Walker director, I wasn't allowed to attend the meeting but Bob and I were asked to ensure that we were available.

When we arrived, we were put in a side room for 15 minutes and were then told that Hills had been sold to Nomura, who had paid the £700million in cash from their own funds, without resorting to a bank syndicate. They were going to organise that later. This was a highly unusual way of proceeding and a high-risk one because there was no certainty that banks would agree to refinance the business, particularly if senior management weren't on board. However, Nomura were an enormous financial organisation and the method enabled deals to be done quickly, which gave them a big advantage over most other buyers because putting a bank syndicate together is a complex and time-consuming exercise.

Having told us the board's decision and that Nomura had completed the deal, Sir Brian Goswell produced a document for Bob and I to sign, regarding the way we were to run the business over the next period of time. It was highly restrictive and impractical and, if carried out to the letter, damaging to the business. It probably reflected Nomura's concern that Hill's management might be hostile but if we signed it we wouldn't be able to run the business properly.

I asked Goswell if he had read it. He said he had. We asked if he had challenged the practicality of its contents but he hadn't. He was another typical Brent Walker chairman of this period. He had the ability and intellect to do a good job but struck both me and Bob as lacking commitment, not prepared to get into the detail of things, and only too willing to go with the flow. We were feeling disappointed and tired and I told him what I thought of him, that we'd built the business up by our efforts with numbers betting and so on and now he wanted us to sign a piece of paper to stop us doing our jobs, without even challenging it.

When the chairmanship of William Hill had come up, following the departure of Sir Keith Bright, both Bob and I, and the two non-executives on the board, had voted against Goswell, already chairman of Brent Walker, becoming Hill's chairman. Having lived through Bright's reign, we felt it was time to have a chairman who knew something about the business and had an interest in it. We thought that Michael Blackburn was the best man for the job and proposed him but Standard Chartered, the lead bank, wanted a Brent Walker nominee.

The vote was three for and three against, with Blackburn and Goswell abstaining – stalemate. We were then threatened that additional directors would be appointed to secure a majority. Another vote was taken, with the same result, the meeting was closed and another called for a few days later. This time we were told that, if the stalemate continued, we would all be removed from the board. We had anticipated this and, as it was clear that we couldn't win, we abstained. So Goswell was voted in by a vote of three for and five abstentions, which must be something of a record for any new chairman. William Hill acquired yet another chairman who knew nothing about the business.

Why the banks were so insistent on having Goswell as chairman, and why he was so keen, remains a mystery, because he didn't turn up for most of the board meetings. Blackburn ended up occupying the chair more often than Goswell. In the end, Blackburn wrote to Goswell to say that he thought it was inappropriate for the chairman to miss so many meetings, although I suspect that he put it a little more strongly than that.

While we were arguing with Goswell about the document Nomura wanted us to sign, the Nomura team were in a neighbouring room. We were told that they'd like to see us but we had already decided that, if that happened, we would not meet them because we would be in the wrong frame of mind. So we told Goswell to tell them that we wouldn't see them that night – it was already early morning – but would meet them the next day.

By now we were starving. We had worked late, until 9.00pm, and were on our way to get something to eat when we got the call to meet the board at the offices of Close Brothers, at midnight. We knew we were going to be told which bid had been successful, feared the worst, and no longer felt hungry. If the *Sunday Telegraph* was right, we could soon be out of work.

We made our way towards Close Brothers' offices and sat in a nearby 24-hour diner, Fat Harry's, drinking coffee until the witching hour. At about 11.30pm my mobile phone rang. It was Donald Mackenzie of CVC, phoning from the south of France. He said we must have lost. When I asked why, he replied that when you win they want to know where the money is and they hadn't called to ask. We knew that Nomura's bid must have been successful but clung to the hope that Brent Walker wouldn't agree to it without the management being committed. We had prepared ourselves for losing, and what might follow, and had spoken to solicitor David Wootton from Allen & Overy, who had agreed to stay at his office in case we needed immediate advice. After we had been told the news, and given the document to sign, we took it to Wootton's office.

All the big City firms have their own 24-hour kitchens, probably because they are constitutionally incapable of finalising an agreement during normal working hours. At 1.00am, they rustled up a roast chicken dinner and bottle of wine for us. Champagne didn't seem appropriate. We showed Wootton the document that we wouldn't sign and he drafted a response, explaining why we couldn't sign it in its present form, and sought clarification of the details. We then faxed it to Nomura and set about drafting an announcement to be put on the screens in our betting shops when they opened in the morning, saying it was business as usual. Then we went back to our flats and went to bed, our minds in turmoil. It was 3.00am.

After very little sleep, Bob and I set off for work really early the next day. The City pages of teletext carried the headline, "Nomura buys William Hill." It had done so using a new company, The Grand Bookmaking Company. It didn't seem very grand to me. I took a large felt tip pen and wrote a big notice with just two words on it – "AH SO" – and drew a picture of the rising sun and stuck it on the outside of my office door. At 8.00am, I rang Nomura but couldn't get hold of anyone so I finalised the draft statement for William Hill's staff to reassure them, explaining who had bought us and that they would be unaffected. It was business as usual although it didn't seem usual to me.

At about 8.30am I received a telephone call from Goswell, to tell me that he thought I was about to make a terrible mistake by not agreeing to work for Nomura. I replied that I'd explained the previous night that it wasn't the right time to talk to them. We had never said we weren't going to work for them and, in any case, we had a contract and would honour it, whatever the circumstances. I repeated what I had told him the night before: that we would have got off on the wrong foot if we had met them there and then.

To be fair to Brent Walker and the banks, we did get a big exit bonus. The deal had been that, when William Hill was sold, we would get a payment based on the selling price but it didn't kick in until £600million. That seemed alright at the time but then the National Lottery came along and the business probably wasn't worth £400million. Management had no incentive because to get the value up to £600million seemed almost impossible. With numbers betting, we did it, but that couldn't have been predicted at the time so they talked to us about changing the scheme.

Brent Walker agreed that, instead of the bonus starting at a sale price of £600million, it would start at £500million, with a cap at £650million. When it eventually became clear that we were going to be sold for more than that, with the support of the no-doubt-grateful banks, they removed the cap. As with all sale bonuses, it was paid for out of shareholders' funds, in this case the bank syndicate.

At around 9.30am that morning, Ray Hart rang from Nomura, cleared the announcements to the staff that we had sent them earlier in the morning, and we set off to meet him to discuss the unsigned document. Hart explained that the document was just to protect their position overnight and for the first few weeks and asked what we didn't like about it. As we were getting into the detail, Guy Hands popped in. We said, "Look, we can't sign this." He asked, "Are you going to carry on running the business as normal for the time being?" We said, "Yes." Then he said, "Forget the document." He asked whether there was anything else we wanted to talk about. We thought he was alluding to management incentives but we had already decided not to raise the subject at this stage. We thought that if Nomura had taken a chance and bought William Hill without our commitment, it wasn't a good time for us to be negotiating a management deal.

Evidently the day after Nomura bought us, they were in touch with Matthew Collins of Bankers Trust who had organised the bank funding arrangements for CVC and Cinven's bid. Nomura wanted to use the same arrangements. Matthew telephoned Bob and I and asked if we objected to the proposal. There seemed no point in objecting so we thanked Matthew for having asked us, told him that he owed us nothing and that business was business. You win some and you lose some. We had lost but there was no reason why he should.

We had spurned Nomura because we didn't think their funding proposal matched ours and, when the deal was done, they used our banking proposal because they couldn't better it. Would we have gone with them if we had known that they would use our banking arrangements? Maybe, maybe not. We will never know.

Guy Hands was a really nice person and so was his wife, Julia. In the summer, we invited them to William Hill's box at Royal Ascot. Julia said, "They must have given Guy the wrong suit." There he was, super wealthy, he'd hired his outfit from Moss Bros, and it seemed to be three sizes too big. His top hat was balanced precariously on his ears, and the bottoms of his trousers were in concertina folds. He looked like a member of the Crazy Gang and we all had such a laugh, including Guy. They didn't know much about racing but, using *Timeform* and a little intuition, still managed to back the first three winners. Lucky Guy.

When a company like Nomura buy a business they should let the existing management run it. You have to have faith in managers and if you don't and don't like the way they are running the business, then you have to get rid of them. What you mustn't do is keep them but try to tell them how to run the business.

After Nomura sold us, Guy Hands told me that I was the only chief executive of a company he had bought of whom he hadn't got rid of. I thought that was a great compliment. I told him, tongue in cheek, that he was the only chairman of William Hill who I hadn't got rid of. Guy was a good man. When I asked him if he wanted to use the William Hill box at Wembley Stadium when there was a pop concert on, he invited nine extremely ill children from Great Ormond Street Hospital and their nurses to see the Spice Girls. Those who were able to, went down and met Emma Bunton, 'Baby Spice'. Nomura produced a small album for each of the children, to remember the day.

Ray Hart was a nice man too. On a personal level, I got on well with him but not with his management style. Having previously worked for a large conglomerate, Ray wanted to know every little thing that we were doing. I had to report to him continually, which, after my freedom under Brent Walker, I found irksome. That summer, though, just after the World Cup, on which we enjoyed record turnover and profits, he did suggest a deal for management of the type but not the amount that we would have had if CVC and Cinven had taken over. The fact that, after nothing had been said for several months, a deal was suddenly mentioned, told us that they must already be contemplating selling.

They'd only had us for about six months but there were stories that Japanese banks and Nomura were suffering from the economic downturn. The offer was pretty low but we didn't say no. Ray was about to go on holiday and was in a rush. He came over late one night, left some documents for us to look at and said it was money for nothing.

Bob and I resorted to one of our two most frequently used strategies when we found ourselves in situations we didn't like, weren't sure how to deal with or were unsure as to how strong our negotiating position was: we played for time. We would either do nothing in a display of masterly inactivity or, as in this case, ask for several points to be clarified. Every time Ray tried to pin us down, we asked for more details. We were like a sponge: the more we were pushed, the more we gave, but we resumed our position as soon as the pushing stopped. It's difficult to negotiate when the other side doesn't respond. We didn't ask for a better deal or more money; we just kept asking for more information.

At around the same time, Bob and I were asked to go to the USA to do a roadshow to help refinance £150million of debt by way of a £150million sterling bond to potential investors. I believe it was the first sterling offering in the USA.

At the end of one day's presentations, in Philadelphia, we were tired out and just wanted a quick snack, somewhere nearby. Someone said what we needed was a Philadelphia sandwich and that they knew where to get the best. So we piled into a limousine, with Matthew Collins of Bankers Trust, thinking we'd be going a couple of blocks. Thirty minutes later, we were still driving and still hadn't arrived. Eventually, the car pulled up outside a long, glass-fronted diner on a small parade of shops. There was a sign in the window, "Winner of the Philadelphia Sandwich Competition". We were all in our suits and ties and polished shoes and the diner was full of truck drivers. We must have looked ridiculous.

"Yeah, what ya all want?"

"Six Philadelphia sandwiches and six beers, please." Bang, down came the bottles of beer, tops off, but no glasses.

Most people were sitting on bar stools and four were at a table. "You four, off, they want to eat their sandwiches." Then the sandwiches arrived. They were long rolls, full of meat – lots of meat – melted cheese, onions and mushrooms. So we got our Philadelphia sandwiches, the best in town. I am not sure Matthew Collins had ever experienced anything quite like it, especially when the fat dripped down on to his expensive suit.

When we got back to London, Ray Hart had left Nomura, and the personnel director took over the negotiations about a management deal. "What is it you want?" he asked. We settled on a figure substantially higher than the one Ray Hart had proposed but nowhere near what we'd have got if CVC and Cinven had bought William Hill. It was a percentage of the amount by which the company's value had increased since Nomura bought it. The deal was tied up within one or two days. Very quickly after that, Nomura made us aware of their decision to sell William Hill and we moved into float mode for the second but not the final time.

*

Officially, we were now owned by the Grand Bookmaking Company

Limited, which was owned by Nomura. Within three months, Ladbrokes had bought Corals. That was on New Year's Eve 1997. Nomura were on the phone straight away. I told them that it would mean that Ladbrokes would be the biggest bookmaker for ever, we would always be second best, and we had to oppose the takeover. Ladbrokes had 1,904 shops in the UK and Corals had 833. We had 1,515. Even before we submitted our case to the Monopolies and Mergers Commission, I thought there was no way the merger should be allowed to stand and, in my opinion, the BHB made a blunder in supporting it. They put in a submission backing the merger because Ladbrokes had agreed to sell 134 shops to the Tote. It was an untenable position for the BHB to have adopted.

While the MMC had a look at that takeover, we were making real progress with our business. In March 1998, we launched a telephone service for non-UK customers, based on the Isle of Man. In May we launched a tax-free internet service for overseas customers, from the same base.

Right from the start, Nomura had been insistent that we embrace the internet, which at the time I wasn't greatly excited about. I would have waited. I couldn't see how internet betting could take over from betting shops and telephone betting but they really drove us, rightly as it turned out, and we got a site running for the World Cup, in June 1998, and took £500,000 on it. That convinced me that internet betting was here to stay and represented a big opportunity for William Hill.

That year's World Cup was tremendous for us. Overall, we had turnover of £40million and the results were pretty good, with France beating Brazil in the final. Numbers betting and amusement with prizes machines and the World Cup meant that Hill's profits would leap up to over £90million that year. Nomura had only owned us for 10 months when, that August, they appointed Warburg Dillon Read to advise them on a stock market flotation, with a valuation of £800million to £900million mentioned. That would have been between £100million and £200million profit in about a year. Not bad if you can get it.

When you are going to float, you appoint advisers, draw up a prospectus, and give presentations to financial institutions likely to take up some of the shares. Warburg had a department purely to organise presentations and they did it very well. It was very hectic and intense.

So we started on our roadshow, here and in the USA, making presentations about the business over and over again, sometimes one to one, at other times to small groups, at breakfasts, lunches and dinners. We didn't get to eat much ourselves because we were too busy making the presentation and answering questions while the analysts and fund managers were eating. Apparently, giving them a free meal was the accepted way for drawing them in, whether they'd any intention of investing or not.

There were an awful lot of presentations, many of them one-on-one to big institutions. It was quite demanding and after we'd given the same presentation 66 times, mind-numbingly boring. The exercise was packed into a few weeks, so there were private cars and private jets and stretch-limos waiting for us at airports to get us round in double quick time, real jet-set stuff. We'd get back from the USA on an overnight flight, be taken by car to the Savoy Hotel, shower, shave, and be on our way in an hour to give yet another presentation. It was difficult not to sound jaded.

There was a stark difference between the UK and the USA. You'd visit a big financial institution in London and there might be ten or twelve people sitting around a table. One of them would look as if he had left school the previous day and it frequently seemed that not many had bothered to read the documentation. We'd give our presentation and then they'd ask the most stupid questions. "Why don't you sell beer in betting shops?" Or they'd ask questions that were clearly answered in the prospectus. It was shameful but it was a regular occurrence.

You won't be surprised when I say that I found it very hard not to be rude to them and occasionally was rude to them. These highly-paid people were going to decide whether or not to invest many millions of other people's money and, in my view, they were unprofessional in their approach. They called themselves professionals, they probably prided themselves on being professionals, I expect they had been to the right schools and had letters after their names but I didn't think they were doing their job properly. I didn't have much time for most of them and I am sure it showed.

Just occasionally, people would say, "We've read your document from beginning to end, we don't need you to give your presentation, we'd just like to ask a few questions." I found that refreshing but it didn't happen very often. When we went to the USA, it was very different. Everyone who had signed up to see the presentation had usually read the documents. They wanted to see how we talked about our business and they didn't ask questions off the cuff: they'd thought them out. The Americans were very different and it was very interesting.

From quite early on, Bob and I could see that there were problems with the flotation. Guy Hands had made it clear that he didn't want to sell William Hill but Nomura did and they were going to sell 100 per cent of it. That was unusual. In these situations the seller normally keeps maybe 30 per cent of the shares for at least a year or two after the flotation to demonstrate their continuing faith in the business. However, in our case, Warburg had advised Nomura that they could sell 100 per cent and that was the right approach and that, if Nomura kept some shares, people would know that they weren't going to hold on to their shareholding longer than they had to and that the 'overhang' would depress the share price. People would be more likely to invest if Nomura sold the lot straight away. That, I am sure, was a mistake.

Investors were told that the price would be between £840million and £900million. I thought Hills was worth more than that but, in terms of our appeal to investors, we fell between two stools. Sitting on one were the investors who wanted growth and on the other were those who wanted a good dividend.

People were asking us where the growth was coming from. This isn't a business where growth is easy to predict. There was no obvious new legislation coming along to open up new markets. All we could do was point to our record of growth over the past few years, show that we had grown through innovation, and point to the potential of the internet. Neither Bob nor I felt that we could promise high growth, although our pre-tax profits had gone from £39.3million in 1995, to £49.5million, to £76.4million and were expected to be about £93.5million in 1998. We thought that was pretty good evidence that we knew how to build and grow a business.

It was a high-cashflow business and we were offering to pay a dividend of about 3.25 per cent, which wasn't enough to satisfy those who wanted high dividends. They were asking us what we were going to do with the money the prospectus showed we would build up. We didn't have a straightforward answer. Maybe buy more betting shops, or pay an extraordinary dividend. But the investors for growth didn't want their money back when they'd only just given it to us, while the investors for dividends didn't want excessive investment, they wanted higher dividends. Bob kept saying that our message was confused: we were not promising growth and were not offering a high dividend. We felt it wasn't working but it was a new experience for us and Warburg kept reassuring us that it was going fine. In reality, it wasn't.

On the Tuesday of the final week, 16 February 1999, we went to Warburg's offices for a meeting attended by Nomura. Warburg told them, for the first time, that they were going to have difficulty getting the float away at the indicated price. Nomura's representatives expressed shock, and replied that all they could do was relay the message to Guy Hands.

Bob Lambert and I then went to the airport to catch a plane to Italy for a presentation the next day. It was a wasted journey. The people there had no interest whatsoever in investing in William Hill and were almost doing Warburg a favour turning up. While we were there, we heard that Warburg had advised Nomura to cut the share offer price to below 155p a share, which meant below the £840million which was the bottom end of the range. We asked Warburg if that was right and they said, "No."

When we got off the plane in London on the Wednesday evening, we phoned Nomura. "Was it right that they had been advised to cut the price?" They replied, "Yes." We said, "Well, if you are thinking of doing that, it has implications for the management and we need to come and see you tomorrow morning."

Bob and I intended to object strongly. We were fed up with Warburg and what we thought was their mismanagement of the process and were going to tell Nomura that if they were going to cut the price we needed to renegotiate the management deal. They came back two hours later and said they'd told Warburg that under no circumstances would they cut the price. They either proceeded at the present price, or aborted the float. So there was no need to meet.

We carried on with the final rounds of presentations. Mid-morning on Thursday, the last day of presentations, we got a message to say that Nomura had agreed to cut the price. Instead of a minimum of 155p a share, it was going to be 135p a share, valuing William Hill at £780million. One of Warburg's people said to us, "It's great news. We can get it away now." I replied, "What's great about it? We have failed to sell the business for what we think it's worth." To my mind, Warburg were going to get paid for selling Hills at a price substantially below the one at which they had valued the company.

Needless to say, Bob and I were very unhappy. We couldn't get anyone at Nomura, so we went off to do another presentation and not in a great frame of mind. Neither Bob nor I had thought the presentations had been going well but Warburg had kept insisting that they were, and that this was all normal; the demand would come in late. Now they were panicking. Cutting the price was their only way out. Bob and I considered packing up and not attending the final presentations. However, as we were so close to the end of the series, we decided to carry on, with a presentation at Barings before lunch and one at Lazards in the afternoon.

We were on our way to Barings when the phone rang. It was Nomura. "Where are you?" the man asked. We said, "In a car with

Warburgs, on our way to Barings." He said, "Stop the car and walk to somewhere you can't be heard. Guy Hands wants to talk to you privately. He's in Barbados. He'll phone you shortly."

So I stopped the car, walked round the corner, out of sight and earshot, and waited for my phone to ring. It rang. "Are you where no one can hear you or see your reaction?" asked Guy. "Yes." Then Guy told me that, to prevent the float collapsing early and keep Warburg working, he'd agreed to cut the price but that he had no intention of floating the business at the price Warburg were now suggesting. He told me that he had been having talks with Cinven and CVC and they had agreed to buy the business for £825million. He proposed paying the management bonus as if the business had been floated at 155p a share, the bottom of the price range. The conditions were that Bob and I agreed to carry on working for William Hill, which was the only basis on which Cinven and CVC, and the existing bank syndicate, were prepared to proceed. We were to meet with them later that night to update them on the state of the business. I accepted.

"Don't tell Warburg," Guy said. "We are going to let them carry on thinking everything is all right."

So we carried on to Barings and did our presentation. At the end, one of the Barings' people said, "I've heard that the price is coming down. How do you and Mr Lambert feel about it, and how does it affect your bonus?" I said, "Well, at that price, there isn't any bonus and we won't feel anything about it because we aren't going to be there. We're very unhappy. We'll be resigning." Barings' team were stunned and Warburg's man was dumbstruck.

We got back in the car and he said, "You can't do that. No one is going to buy Hills if the management team leave." I replied, "We're not happy. We've been telling you it hasn't been working and you've been telling us that it's fine. Now you've cut the price, without discussing how that will affect us." He said, "We've got to talk about this." I replied, "There's nothing to talk about. Take us on to Lazards to finish and we'll see you in a couple of weeks."

We met Cinven and CVC that night and briefed them on the

business. We already knew their team well because we had worked with them before Nomura stepped in, which speeded things up. Bob and I confirmed that we would stay on and expected other senior managers to do the same. Continuity was always important and Cinven and CVC needed to make sure that the existing bank syndicates would stay in place. Management changes might threaten that. They shook hands with Nomura on their deal and Bob and I shook hands with Cinven and CVC on an agreement that allowed management 10 per cent of the equity. Less than 48 hours later, the formalities had been completed. It is strange to think that, just over a year earlier, they hadn't been prepared to go above £650million and now they were willing to pay £825million; but how right they proved to be.

It was about 2.20pm by the time we'd signed the documents. I said, "Is that it? Good. The 2.25 at Ascot's on. Put the television on." A few months later, Donald Mackenzie, CVC's partner, told me that at the time he'd thought, "Oh, God, I've taken on a betting junkie."

The deal was announced later that afternoon and Warburg weren't very pleased. They claimed that, if they'd known that Cinven and CVC were prepared to pay £825million, they would have had a stronger hand when approaching institutions and could have got the float away at the original price. They still hadn't got it right at 135p. When the final applications were counted, the issue was oversubscribed because they had substantially underestimated the demand from private investors. For me, it was a great learning experience, and I emerged from it thinking that, on this occasion, Warburg hadn't done a very good job. Nor had the fund managers who weren't prepared to invest in the company.

We never really found out why institutional investors weren't sufficiently enthused to order sufficient stock in the run-up to the float. Was it envy that Guy Hands might make £100million profit in one year? Did they try to drive the price down, not suspecting that Guy had a back-up exit strategy? Was it that they didn't like or trust the management to produce the goods? Didn't Bob and I sell the business well enough in the presentations? I don't know but what I do know is that their decision cost them, collectively, at least £600million.

I can only say that, with hindsight, I was glad they took the decision they did. It meant that Guy made £100million profit in one year, the management passed 'Go' and got its bonus from Nomura's profit and were still on the Monopoly board and on our way towards 'Go' again. From our point of view, it was the best result there could have been although one we had tried hard to avoid. Lucky John.

CHAPTER NINE
THE BRAT FROM OUTER SPACE

Nomura had pushed me into launching an internet site and it was up and running but not to my satisfaction. It wasn't fast enough and a lot of time and effort was being invested in order to make it faster and more reliable. Cinven and CVC pushed even harder. They felt that we were not growing the customer base quickly enough and that awareness of our site was too low. Much against my marketing instincts but in an effort to raise the site's profile and demonstrate to the financial institutions that we were growing the business, we advertised on the sides of buses in Leeds and London and several other major cities until I got so unhappy with the way the site was working, or wasn't working, that I stopped the advertisements.

We then brought in an outside team of specialists to design a new website. When they eventually presented their design, it looked very nice. It was in the shape of a wheel, with different sports in different sections of the wheel. By that point, though, they only had horseracing and football on the wheel.

"How long before we get greyhounds?" I asked. "About three months."

"When will we get golf?" I asked. "About six months."

The text was light blue on a dark blue background. There is a reason why they don't print books using light blue print on dark blue pages. You can't read it as well as black on white. I started to lose my temper.

"I don't want it to look pretty," I told the designer. "I want punters to be able to read it easily. I want it to move fast and I want to be able to add new sports within days, not months. This is useless, bloody useless."

The discussion got a bit heated.

"You think I'm just a poncy designer, don't you?" the designer said.

"No, I don't think you're just a poncy designer," I told him. "I know you are. This is totally impractical. You're out. We'll do it ourselves."

So the William Hill team sat down and started to design a site using a simple template, because a computer doesn't know whether it's a horse race or a golf match. All it knows is that there's a bet, there's a price and there's a result. We did a complete re-design, we had every sport on it, we re-launched the site in August 1999, and it worked as well as anyone else's but it didn't work quickly enough for me. It was prone to slow down at crucial times, although the development team were working hard to improve it. We invested in bigger computers and other pieces of equipment and each change brought an improvement but also exposed another problem. It was like peeling an onion without ever reaching the middle.

In the run-up to the 2000 Grand National, with the site getting better and faster, we took the bull by the horns and advertised in every national newspaper, "No queues on the web." As soon as the site got busy, it fell over. This time it was the links to the Switch card system that couldn't cope, leaving hundreds of potential customers with their transactions frozen in cyber space.

The real problem was that bookmakers were trying to do something completely new. There were plenty of sites that regularly had thousands of hits but very, very few which also carried out thousands of transactions, and even fewer were attempting to carry out thousands of transactions per minute and transfer money by Switch cards at the same time. It wasn't just the Grand National. Every Saturday at 3.00pm, just before kick-off time for football, the site slowed right down or froze and we were struggling to find out where the bottle-necks were. If online betting was to grow, and we were to be a major player, this couldn't go on.

Until this experience we had always developed our own systems, and very successfully, but we had underestimated the complexities of the new technologies used on the internet. We were learning the hard way, through our pocket, and the development team conclud-ed that we needed specialist help. So, for the first time ever, we called in consultants from a wide variety of top companies – IBM and Siemens and other specialists in website transactions. They found a whole series of problems, some major, some minor, but all damaging our online performance. In the end, the specialists came up with hundreds of recommendations to improve the site, which we then set about implementing, one by one, over a period of time. And all the time, there was a lot of pressure on me; pressure from the internet operations team and pressure from Cinven and CVC to make more progress.

Ralph Topping, our online operations manager, and his team wanted to put a lot of content on the site, such as horseracing form and football league tables. I kept saying no: it would slow the site down and my experience of punters told me that, if they hadn't already found that kind of information elsewhere, they wouldn't come to us for it. What we needed more than anything else was a site that worked reliably, all the time, and was quick, very quick. Until our site was the fastest site there was, I didn't want to put any extra content on it at all.

Cinven and CVC were pushing me to do deals with other busi-nesses, both online and off. Just before they bought us, Morgan Grenfell Private Equity, part of Deutsche Bank, had bought Corals for

£390million. At the end of 1999, Corals bought Eurobet, an internet betting company, turned themselves into Coral Eurobet, and spent a lot of money marketing and promoting their site. In March 2000, they launched a UK site, eurobet.co.uk, and, at the same time, announced that they had become Manchester United's exclusive online betting partner with a hotlink to the team's official website, and lead sponsor of Arrows Formula One team. They were making deals and establishing partnerships. What were we doing?

It was the height of the dot com boom. Everyone on the net was doing all sorts of deals with each other and we weren't doing deals because I was refusing to do any. It seemed to me that the business models of most sites were unsustainable and the deals they were asking us to sign up to were ridiculous; yet people were signing up to them.

Bill Haygarth, the director of our internet operation, and Cinven and CVC wanted us to sign up to 'bounty' deals. These were deals offered by sports content providers who were getting tens of thousands of hits on their sites but had no income. In return for a permanent link from their site to William Hill's, they wanted an upfront payment plus a hefty share of all future profits, typically 50 per cent of any profits from customers who had opened an account with us as a result of using the link from their site.

This seemed to me to be commercial madness but others were signing and people on our team wanted me to agree to deals of this kind. They argued that I just didn't understand: this was the way of doing business on the web; it was the new business model and I was living in the past. It was the way of the web. If we were to succeed we had no choice. This was the way forward.

I said, "Look. It may be the way other people are doing it but we're not going to. It isn't sensible and it won't work. We aren't giving anyone a share of our profits for any period of time, ever, in order to open an account." My reasoning was that the bricks and mortar brand names, well-known names, would eventually win out and that punters on the internet were no different to punters elsewhere. They still wanted convenience and the best prices. Convenience on the internet equalled the speed of the site. All we had to do was make our site the fastest, offer competitive odds and eventually the punters would find us. When they did, we would have them forever.

None of the content provider companies had any real income. What they did was present information for which people didn't pay. They had some advertising but most of it was from other similar sites who also didn't have any income. I couldn't understand why the companies running these sites had such huge valuations placed on them. It reminded me of an earlier experience with betting shops, when we had sometimes been outbid for shop leases by the Sock Shop and Tie Rack, and I would ask how they could possibly afford to pay more rent than us, selling socks and ties — we must be in the wrong business. We weren't; they couldn't afford to and both companies later got into terrible trouble. The internet boom was like that. It didn't seem to make sense and, as it turned out, it wasn't sensible.

The management at Coral Eurobet paid fortunes to sponsor Arrows, who rarely made the cut in Formula One races, and one of their senior executives boasted to me about having advertising on off-shore power boats. What good was that? Did people train their binoculars on off-shore power boats, see the name 'Coral Eurobet' in the distance, and dash off to put a bet on the internet with them?

I resisted all the pressure from within William Hill and from our venture capitalist backers to do these deals. Although CVC and Cinven kept querying my decisions, crucially, and in my view properly, they never overruled them, which, as the owners of the business, they could have done. The thing that mattered to me was getting our website to work and work quickly, and that's what I insisted we concentrate on. It goes back to what I have said before about running a business. If we'd had a vote about doing internet deals and paying a share of our profits to appear on other sites, I'd have lost the vote. In the event, that was academic, because I was allowed to run the business in the way I wanted. If my decisions turned out to be wrong, Cinven and CVC could remove me, but fortunately they didn't turn out to be wrong.

Until then, I hadn't had a personal computer at home but decided I ought to get one, so that I could cast a customer's eye over our website, as well as have access to *Raceform Interactive*. The experts at work selected a top of the range laptop for me, I had *Raceform Interactive* installed and, the next day, went to Mustique on holiday with Chris, who became my wife several years after Jenny's death. At the hotel, when I tried to get on the internet and download *Raceform* data, the screen went blue and the computer shut down.

I phoned Mark Nelson at *Raceform* and Jamie Bladd in our computer department for help. In fact, I kept phoning them for help, several times every day. Eventually, Chris said, "Don't you think you should go down and find out how much the phone calls are costing?" I said, "No," but Chris persisted. "I really think you should find out." So I went down to the reception desk and asked. "Yes, sir. So far it's £850." I wasn't on the phone much after that.

When I got home, Mark quickly sorted the problems out and buying a laptop proved to be one of the best things I've ever done. It meant that, with help from Mark, and from Jamie, Kevin Middleton and Nick Copley in our computer department, I was able to keep on top of internet developments. It was invaluable. Wherever I went, whether it was in the UK or abroad, one of the first things I did when I arrived at a hotel was to get on the internet and see how well our website was working. I was constantly ringing the office to tell them that it wasn't working quickly enough. Sometimes I'd try to register to open an account and see how long that took.

I couldn't see past the fact that all we had to do, once our site was right, was to get a customer to visit it once. If the site was good enough, he'd use it, and carry on using it. Slowly but surely, as we implemented all the recommendations and upgrades, the site got more and more reliable and faster and faster, and business started to grow at an increasing pace. This brought new problems because our office systems could not keep pace with the growth. People were opening accounts, depositing money with a credit card and then claiming that the account wasn't theirs. Most of these problem cases were from the

USA, which made them very hard to chase up. Other people would deposit money using someone else's card, have a small bet, then ask for the rest to be refunded by cheque, and operations management wasn't picking it up.

We were building up business so fast that the management systems and procedures got left behind. Bob Lambert wanted us to slow down and sort it out but we were in a gold rush and I decided to chase the business rather than let it go somewhere else. I took the view that we could sort the systems' problems out as we went along but that, if we sacrificed new business, it might go somewhere else. It took us six months to deal with the problems and, along the way, we were the victims of a deliberate, £800,000 fraud, most of which we later recovered in court.

When I told the board that we'd lost £800,000, they were naturally concerned but I told them they had to put it in context. It was a one-off system flaw that had been corrected, and the reason we had lost the money was because the business was growing so quickly. Eight hundred thousand pounds was only the equivalent of one or two bad results on a Saturday. By the second year of operation, the systems were sorted out and we were making a profit from our internet site, possibly the only bookmaker in the UK to be doing so, and one of few internet businesses to be doing so.

I suspect that Coral Eurobet would have happily settled for our problems. Their internet business managed to lose £12million on Euro 2000. They were taking on Asian bookmakers for huge sums on each match and asking them to put the bets on the internet to boost that side of the business. They achieved massive turnover but not profits. Their internet operation managed to lose over £19million that year; more than the profit from all their betting shops put together. It was an amazing turn of events but not one I wanted to emulate. They weren't sponsoring Arrows for very long.

Another popular proposal I wasn't very keen on was to focus on the Far East. People told me we should be targeting Hong Kong. Bookmakers were illegal in Hong Kong and it was suggested that all the punters there were crying out for the opportunity to bet with a legal bookmaker. Maybe they would bet with William Hill on the internet. But punters in Hong Kong weren't dying to bet with William Hill, of whom they'd probably never heard, nor with any other legal UK bookmaker.

Illegal doesn't necessarily mean inefficient or unreliable. Hong Kong's illegal bookmakers were giving punters the best prices, providing runners to take their bets, paying out immediately after the result and generally giving a professional service. Hong Kong punters were happy with what they had.

Instead, at the end of 1999, while Corals were buying Eurobet and about to lose a fortune, we launched an online casino, from Antigua. Later, we moved it to the Netherlands Antilles. We recognised the potential of online casino gaming early on and, that October, entered into a deal with CryptoLogic, one of the leading online casino software providers. It made us the first UK bookmaker to have its own casino site. After a slow start, while we acquired the marketing skills needed to promote this new medium, it did extremely well.

Ladbrokes continually tell anyone who will listen that they are the industry leaders, the biggest and the best, which gets to me. All they have been good at in the recent past is spending money buying more betting shops. In reality, they're not even best at that. They've got about 400 more shops than us in the UK and in 2001 we made £1.6million more profit from our shops than they did. In the first half of 2003, we made £3.6million more than Ladbrokes from shops.

In the areas where it isn't about how much money you have been able to spend and where the number of outlets doesn't dictate who has the highest turnover, we are miles in front of them, as the City is finally beginning to appreciate. Since our flotation, the true extent of William Hill's superiority is in the public domain. Our telephone betting business is the clear market leader and that is also true for internet betting and gaming.

In 2001, Ladbrokes made a profit of £3.6million from telephone betting, while we made £15.6million. In the first half of 2003, they made £4.7million; we made £9.1million. It's the same with e-gaming. After losing £10million on it in 2000, Ladbrokes bragged about going into profit the next year but their profit was £2million while ours was £9.2million. They still haven't caught up. In the first half of 2003, their e-gaming profit was £5.1million; ours was £11.3million.

All in all, I find it difficult to see exactly why they think they are the industry leaders.

*

In May 1999, Victor Chandler really put the cat among the pigeons by moving his telephone betting business to Gibraltar and offering 'tax-free' betting to UK customers. Instead of paying the usual 9 per cent deduction, Chandler's clients only had to pay a service charge of 3 per cent.

Overseas-based customers could already bet more or less deduction-free and Chandler wasn't the only bookmaker to have a site off-shore. Ladbrokes also had a base on Gibraltar for their overseas clients and we had one on the Isle of Man but neither of us took bets from UK residents. Victor Chandler's initiative really changed things. Why would UK punters phone a UK-based bookmaker when they could phone Chandler on a free phone number and pay 6 per cent less in deductions than in the UK? Some of the bigger-staking punters were betting with Chandler without any deductions at all.

The Betting Office Licensees Association immediately commissioned a report from Europe Economics, which showed that, if the government didn't do something, the domestic betting industry would shrink alarmingly, and so would government revenue.

In July, I went with Chris Bell, Tom Kelly and others to meet Barbara Roche, the Financial Secretary to the Treasury. We told her that if the Treasury didn't take rapid action and cut betting duty from 6.75 per cent to at least 3 per cent, we would be forced to take our telephone and internet businesses off-shore. We had a duty to our shareholders and there would be no choice. I then told her that this was a real problem, which, one way or another, was going to cost the Treasury revenue. If they cut betting duty they would lose money, most of which would end up with UK bookmakers, but employment would be increased. If they didn't cut duty, then we would move off-shore and they would lose revenue and jobs would also be lost. She told us that, in the short term, nothing could or would be done. The government didn't work like that. We told her that, in that case, we couldn't sit back and watch our businesses decline; we would have to make plans to move off-shore.

Ladbrokes were first out of the blocks and announced a big extension of their operation in Gibraltar. They started to take bets from UK-based clients. Corals did nothing, and neither did the Tote, although, as a government-linked body, the Tote was in a difficult situation.

We couldn't extend our Isle of Man operation to cover UK customers because the local regulations meant that those bets would have been subject to a 6 per cent tax. Our telephone operation was much bigger than anyone else's and we weren't sure that the telephone system in Gibraltar could cope with Hill's business, on top of Ladbrokes' and Chandler's. They were already having problems with staff and accommodation. There was not a lot for staff brought in from the UK to do in their spare time and the Gibraltar government seemed to be getting a bit nervous about more and more bookmakers moving there and upsetting the UK government.

We looked at Malta and Madeira and Liechtenstein and even at a canton in Switzerland but none of them were suitable. It was painfully slow. Then I had an idea. I had recently phoned British Airways to arrange travel insurance for a holiday. An Irish girl had answered the phone. I had asked where she was and she had replied, "Kilkenny." I suddenly realised that when you rang a company, your call was often dealt with by a business call centre somewhere else while the transaction was recorded in the UK. There were legal reasons why we couldn't have a call centre in the UK and pass the bets to an off-shore site but how about having a call centre in Ireland?

In July 1999, betting tax in Ireland was cut to 5 per cent but I thought we could avoid that by passing the bets from the call centre to an offshore site. We could install a computer and a couple of staff in Gibraltar to process the bets. We consulted an Irish barrister, who told us that, provided the person having the bet wasn't resident in Ireland and the bet wasn't paid for in Ireland, nor any returns paid in Ireland, then there was no transaction in Ireland and no duty would be payable there. The transaction and duty would be where the bet was struck.

But when we told the authorities in Gibraltar that we were thinking of having a computer there but the call centre elsewhere, they became very cool about the idea. They wanted to create jobs and didn't want Gibraltar to be seen as just a UK-tax-avoidance location. So we switched our sights to Antigua, which we were already looking at as the base for our online casino. Bill Haygarth was on holiday in Canada at the time. I phoned him and told him not to come home afterwards but to fly to Antigua and not come back until he had an agreement for William Hill to set up as a bookmaker there.

Meanwhile, the Irish Development Agency told us they wouldn't give us any grants to develop a call centre and, when we had a meeting with our UK lawyers and accountants, they threw up one potential problem after another. I got quite exasperated with them and eventually told them, "Look, we are not here to debate whether or not we are going to do this, we are definitely going to do it. Your sole job is to tell us how we are going to do it in the most efficient way. I am not interested in you saying the Irish government might do this or that, we are launching." That was in October 1999.

We then got a letter from the Irish customs department, which, whilst expressing itself satisfied with our proposal, indicated that it was referring the taxation issues to the revenue commissioners, who eventually told us they weren't entirely happy with the proposal.

We still pressed on and our Irish lawyer arranged for me to meet the Irish finance minister, Charlie McCreevy, who enjoyed his racing. He was down to earth, not your usual smooth politician, a countryman, with a broad accent, so broad that I found it difficult to follow what he was saying at times. He had a civil servant with him who made it absolutely clear that he thought what we were proposing was unacceptable.

By then, we'd already found an industrial shed in Athlone where we could put 250 bet positions and all the necessary equipment. On the back of our legal advice, we had already taken a chance and signed the lease and started work, determined to press on regardless and, if necessary, go to court in Ireland.

Because of the attitude of the civil servant, the meeting wasn't going well and, eventually, I said to the minister, "If you don't want us in Ireland then please tell us now and we'll go somewhere else." We didn't actually have anywhere else to go, and were already fitting out the building, so it was lucky that he said, "Of course we want you, we want the jobs." And that was the end of the meeting. We finally obtained planning permission for the building to be used as an office six months after its opening.

Some years later, I met McCreevy at trainer Jonjo O'Neill's stables. He remembered our meeting well and told me that his official had wanted him to turn down our plan. McCreevy had told him, "We aren't so rich we can do without another 200 jobs." We got the shed fitted out, shipped a computer out to Antigua and, three months after we had said we were moving, we were up and running. We'd done a deal with Aer Lingus because although we eventually recruited all the staff locally, to begin with fully experienced staff flew out from Leeds each week. We had no shortage of volunteers. They loved it. A week away from home, husband and kids and double pay to boot. It was down the pub in the evening with the girls, having a laugh. All in all, it was an attractive proposition.

Although our move didn't attract a lot of publicity and doesn't sound dramatic, I regard it as one of William Hill's greatest achievements under my leadership, partly because of the complexity of it. A call centre in Ireland, a bookmaking operation in Antigua, accounts in the Isle of Man, and odds-setting and risk management in Leeds;

all linked together. To have got the whole operation, with all its technical, administrative, political and legal complications, set up and working within three months, and making money from day one, was a considerable feat. It was a great testament to the management, organisational and technical skills of the team at William Hill, and our solution was one that avoided the problems a base in Gibraltar would have created, because in Ireland there were plenty of local people to employ and plenty of cheap daily flights to and from the UK.

*

That summer, Warwick Bartlett, chairman of the British Betting Offices Association, asked if I would speak at the Industry Seminar in January 2000. Neither of us realised how important that invitation would turn out to be. Warwick had just been elected chairman of the Bookmakers' Committee. Chris Bell wanted to be re-elected and encouraged Warwick not to stand but when Warwick phoned me before the election I told him that if he stood, I'd vote for him. I thought it was the right thing to do. When it came to it, Chris stood down.

Warwick is very innovative and the BBOA's Industry Seminar had quickly established itself as one of the highlights of the industry's calendar, always attracting industry leaders to make key speeches and often attracting government ministers to explain their current thinking and policies. Although I had given a lot of presentations to financial institutions, I wasn't used to speaking in public and I don't find it easy either to write a speech or speak off the cuff. So I was tempted to say no. Then I thought, "We are trying to lead the industry at William Hill, and I ought to do it." So I agreed and started to think about a subject.

Victor Chandler had gone abroad, we had met a Treasury minister to urge a cut in betting duty and we were making plans to go offshore. By the time the Seminar arrived, on 18 January 2000, we were eight days away from giving our UK telephone and internet clients tax-free betting through our call centre in Ireland.

The previous November I had been to a conference in Las Vegas where one presenter used a slide showing a rocket with a baby in it. The baby was the baby internet, about to wreak havoc on the world of gambling and taxation. I enjoyed the presentation so much that I phoned the speaker afterwards and got a copy of his slides. That would be the title of my speech, I thought, "The Brat from Outer Space". And I knew what I was going to suggest; the speaker in Las Vegas hadn't mentioned it but it wasn't a new idea. I'd first heard it from Bob Green, the Mecca boss, many years before, and again in 1994, when Will Roseff had put the idea forward, but nothing had come of it: a gross profits tax.

The question we were all asking was, "How can the UK betting industry compete with tax-free betting offshore?" Bookmakers, including me, were calling for betting duty to be cut from 6.75 per cent to 3 per cent but I started to realise that that wasn't the answer. Even at 3 per cent, with levy payments on top of that, we would still have to make deductions from punters' returns. Bookmakers based in the UK still wouldn't be able to compete on equal terms with offshore bookmakers. What we had to do was have zero deductions. It was the only solution. But how?

Obviously, there was no hope of the government agreeing to nil tax, so the answer was to switch to a tax, not on punters' turnover, but on bookmakers' gross profits. We would pay a proportion of what we won, after having scrapped punters' deductions. I'd always thought that it was iniquitous to tax bookmakers on their turnover rather than their profits, while casinos had always been taxed on their gross win. But it was a high-risk strategy. If we moved to zero deductions, how much more would punters bet? If we could get a gross profits tax, would we actually want it? Green had first proposed it but now everything was indicating that this was the right time to really push for it.

I changed the title of my speech to 'Star Wars', and played the music from the film as an attention-grabbing introduction. My speech was the last before lunch. I was pretty nervous. I'm not a natural at public speaking, although I've got better. I told the audience

– leaders of the betting and racing industries, government officials and politicians, the media – "We have to find a solution that removes the incentive for UK residents to bet offshore, while providing an equal incentive for overseas punters to bet with us." The solution was GPT and no deductions. I told the audience that it wasn't the betting industry's policy yet, it wasn't even William Hill's policy yet, it was just a proposal, an idea whose time had come.

It would give the UK betting industry the opportunity to lead the world, would undermine illegal gambling and, although the government would lose revenue in the short-term, in the longer term its tax revenue would increase as the result of the creation of jobs and greater company profits.

"This country," I said, "with its well-regulated, highly-respected betting industry, has a unique opportunity to simultaneously protect and grow its core home market, the betting shops, and emerge as a world leader for sports betting, an exporter of bets and an earner of foreign currency."

The UK can either become a major centre for e-commerce or a Luddite casualty of a new and dynamic era. Wouldn't it be nice if the betting industry, in partnership with the government, led the way? The brat from outer space is only a threat if we treat him as one. He also has the potential to be the greatest opportunity of all time to change things for the better, for everyone. Scrap betting duty as a percentage of punters' turnover, and substitute it with a percentage of bookmakers' gross profits."

The reaction was better than I could have imagined. It made headlines in the *Racing Post* and everyone was talking about it but, in the run-up to the 2000 Budget, two months later, some bookmakers and the racing industry were still calling for a cut in betting duty rather than a switch to GPT. It didn't help that, while the betting industry called for a cut from 6.75 per cent to 3 per cent, the BHB called for a cut to 5 per cent.

My speech hadn't been forgotten, though. It had started a debate and prompted government action. Gordon Brown's Budget speech, on 21 March, didn't mention betting duty but, later that day, a consultation exercise was announced: "Our Stake in the Future: the Modernisation of General Betting Duty for the 21st Century". The consultation was to focus on two options. The first was a betting duty based on the location of the punter, so that bookmakers based offshore would still have to pay duty on bets they took from UK customers. The second option was a tax based on gross profits.

Customs and Excise commissioned research by a team from Nottingham University, led by David Paton, which eventually produced a report, "An Economic Analysis of the Options for Taxing Betting". The Bookmakers' Committee commissioned another report from Europe Economics, "An Assessment of the Options for Modernising Betting Taxation". Both came down in favour of a gross profits tax. Crucially, perhaps, the government-commissioned report was even more bullish about GPT than the report commissioned by the bookmakers. At the Industry Seminar, I had tentatively suggested a GPT of 20 per cent but Europe Economics concluded that, for the UK betting industry to be competitive, the rate must be no more than 15 per cent.

We knew we were making good progress when Gordon Brown delivered a pre-Budget report in November 2000 and announced, "The government believes there is scope for a modernising reform of general betting duty" and referred to GPT as one possibility. An announcement would be made in the 2001 Budget.

Then, on the anniversary of my Industry Seminar speech, Stephen Timms, Financial Secretary to the Treasury, told the 2001 Seminar, "We are prepared to place a bet on the skills and the abilities of the UK betting industry to win in a worldwide marketplace. We want to make sure we bring betting back onshore and welcome a new international market to this country." In my speech I had promised that, if the government was prepared to have a bet on Britain's bookmakers, we would deliver. It looked as if the government was about to back us. I've never known such a constructive dialogue with Customs and Excise as the one we had with them during that period. A lot of the credit for that goes to two of their officials: Frank Tucker and Kevin Kilmurray. They were very positive. We discussed various scenarios and what the effect would be on the betting industry and on tax revenue.

It was still quite a tense time. About a month before the Budget, the Bookmakers' Committee got a letter from Customs asking how we would react to a cut in betting duty to 3 per cent. I remember Alan Ross, Ladbrokes' managing director, saying that, according to his information, GPT was dead, it was definitely going to be a 3 per cent betting duty.

I said, "Maybe, but we shouldn't give up now. We must write back and say that 3 per cent would be better than no change but it wouldn't be the best possible solution." With that rate, we'd still have to have deductions. The only thing that would work was moving to GPT and having zero deductions. In the long run, that would be better for the government. We wrote the letter.

There were also fears about tax evasion. People asked, "How do you know bookmakers won't put winning bets through the system to reduce their gross profits?" You wouldn't know, but how did you know bookmakers weren't keeping bets out of their books at that time to keep turnover figures down? The fact was that the big bookmaking companies couldn't cheat and they accounted for 90 per cent of all tax and levy payments.

A few days before the Budget, we started to hear more encouraging noises. Frank Tucker was discussing what the right rate would be, if there was a GPT system. We had a feeling the government might opt for 20 per cent. We insisted the system wouldn't work if the rate was more than 15 per cent and tried to sell it by pointing out that a 15 per cent tax didn't sound like a reduction from a 6.75 per cent tax.

With two days to go, a press officer from the Treasury asked what we would say after the Budget if the Chancellor announced a gross profits tax. Hills, Ladbrokes, Corals and BOLA were asked to submit draft press releases. That was easy. On behalf of William Hill I said it was great news, good for customers, good for British racing, good for bookmakers and good for the government. It would bring business in from overseas and create jobs. It was a win, win, win situation.

When Gordon Brown stood up to deliver his Budget speech, on 7 March 2001, we still weren't sure he was going to do it. In the context of the whole Budget, it was a very minor thing but it was major to us. It only took him a few seconds to say, "Following our consultation with the betting and gaming industry over the impact of internet trading, I have decided from 1 January to abolish betting duty, which has been in existence ever since betting shops were legalised. I have agreed that the tax on bookmakers' gross profits will be 15 per cent, which the leading bookmakers have agreed not to pass on to their customers. So by 1 January no one will have to pay a tax on their bets."

I thought it was wonderful, amazing. How often does the government agree to a tax change like that? It was a great day, one of the best and proudest of my career. I hadn't thought of GPT first but my speech at the Industry Seminar had launched the campaign. It was the right idea at the right time We had promised to return our businesses to the UK and to abolish deductions to punters. For betting shop customers, it meant deduction-free betting for the first time since 1966. Don Quixote may have been right. Another windmill had bitten the dust.

*

New Year's Day 2002 was the target date for the switch to GPT but it was understood that, if the necessary preparations could be completed in time, the changeover could come earlier. In July, the Treasury announced that 6 October would be the date when betting duty and deductions would be abolished.

I had started my career in bookmaking at a time when there were no deductions and to have been the catalyst for them being scrapped was tremendous. It was fantastic for bookmakers, for punters, and for racing. There has rarely been as exciting a day for everyone in the industry and for its customers, as 6 October. There was a real carnival atmosphere at William Hill. We celebrated with a nice cup of tea.

Whatever the BHB claim, the main reason racing's income has gone up since Peter Savill became BHB chairman in 1998 is because of the introduction of GPT. I've heard him claim that GPT was a BHB proposal and was in the BHB's Financial Plan but it wasn't their proposal and it wasn't in the Financial Plan. If the BHB was so keen on GPT, what did it do about it after the Plan appeared in January 1998? What they did was say they would only support it if we agreed to support the introduction of betting terminals into pubs.

I never really understood what the Financial Plan was about. The BHB's own auditors criticised it and were replaced for their honesty. I thought it was a poor and flawed document. It wasn't a Financial Plan, it was just a plan to raise money. It said that racehorse owners weren't getting enough prize money because prize money only covered 24 per cent of their costs and should cover 50 per cent. Why should it cover 50 per cent, apart from the fact that it would put British owners ahead of those in France and the USA, countries where circumstances were entirely different?

As I said when I addressed the BHB's annual general meeting in 2002, what about costs? The problem isn't only prize money, it's the cost of training compared to other countries. You can't compare training costs here with those in the USA, or Hong Kong, where everyone trains at the track, there are virtually no travelling expenses and meetings can last 48 days. That is totally different from having trainers in Scotland sending horses to run at Lingfield, or trainers in Newmarket paying to use the gallops. That is one of the main reasons why owners are worse off in this country.

If it was a proper plan, the BHB would have started by looking at what it wanted the racing industry to look like. How many horses? How many all-weather racecourses? What kind of races? Then the Plan would consider how they were going to get there. Even though I'm a racehorse owner myself, I don't think owners should have a seat on the BHB. They are customers and it doesn't matter how much they may have paid to own racehorses, they are still customers not producers.

I paid a lot of money to buy a Bentley but it doesn't make me part of the motor industry and, if I bought 100 Bentleys, I still wouldn't be given a seat on their board. I have never heard a compelling argument for owners being regarded as part of the racing industry. They are not. They are important customers of the racing industry and they should lobby the industry for the things they want but they shouldn't be sitting on the board which runs the industry.

When Peter Savill was working on the Plan, he courted Chris Bell quite extensively. Eventually there was a meeting, attended by Savill, Tristram Ricketts, Chris, myself, and others. We sat around a round table and Savill started to tell us about the Plan, which none of us had seen apart from Chris.

Savill said there had been a couple of minor changes since Chris had seen the Plan but nothing of significance. Chris had apparently told him that he was in support of the proposals or, at least, he hadn't said he wasn't, which led Savill to believe he was – that was Chris's style. I was challenging nearly everything Savill said and getting really aggressive and the meeting ended rather acrimoniously.

Later, when Chris examined these minor changes, what had been changed was a section about who should provide racing with the additional £105million the Plan claimed it needed. The earlier version that Chris had seen stated, "It would be unreasonable to expect bookmakers to pay." In the later version, that had gone. Part of the £105million, the final Plan said, should come from "an increase in the contribution from betting", with an extra 1.75 per cent of betting turnover contributed. For bookmakers it was hardly a minor change and it changed Chris's view. He couldn't believe it and I am sure felt that he had been badly misled.

By the time Gordon Brown announced the end of betting duty, the BHB was working on a commercial deal with bookmakers to replace the levy system, which the government had announced it intended to scrap. The BHB was all in favour of ending the levy system and replacing it with one based on the sale of data rights, which seemed premature to me because, apart from the advantages, including tax advantages, of the levy system, the BHB still hadn't established that the data rights were theirs to sell.

They started by asking William Hill to pay for the use of their data on our internet site. This was not covered by any of the existing agreements so, if the BHB owned the rights, we certainly needed a licence in order to use them. But we were advised that the legal situation was not as clear cut as the BHB believed it to be. They took us to court and won, with a judgement comprehensively in their favour. We then appealed to the High Court for the matter to be referred to the European Court for clarification. The High Court agreed but not before declaring that, if they had determined the case, they would have found in the BHB's favour. We are still awaiting a ruling and until one is issued, the BHB cannot be certain that they own the relevant data rights.

In fact, the European Court has since been asked to deal with several similar cases from different countries, cases where courts in different countries have taken different views. Quite what the BHB will do if the levy disappears and then the European Court finds against them, leaving them with no exploitable data rights, no one at the BHB or DCMS has yet explained.

After the 2001 Budget, it seemed crystal clear to me that any deal between the BHB and betting industry had to be based on gross profits. True to form, led by Savill, the BHB announced that they would never agree to a levy based on gross profits: any deal must be based on turnover. Having claimed to have recommended a gross profits based system to the government, the BHB now insisted that it was not good enough for them.

Between June and October, we had a series of meetings with Savill. At the first, there was no agenda. At the second, we produced an agenda and were told that the BHB had commissioned a report on our profits, which we wouldn't be allowed to see. We tried to point out that a turnover-based levy set at the same figure for everyone would be highly discriminatory against businesses with low gross profits, such as internet, telephone and racecourse bookmakers. We were told, firmly, that payments would be based on turnover and if we didn't like it, we should go to the Office of Fair Trading – that's what it was there for. At the third meeting, we were told what the rate of payment for data rights was going to be – 2.5 per cent of turnover. Since there were no real negotiations taking place, I didn't go to that meeting.

William Hill subsequently submitted a complaint to the OFT, as did most other major companies and trade associations in the betting industry. Our complaint was based on the fact that the rate of 2.5 per cent represented an abuse of the BHB's monopoly position and that basing a charge on turnover had a different impact on different businesses. It was therefore discriminatory and unfair. The complaint triggered a wider investigation of the racing industry by the OFT.

There seemed to us to be no hope of a levy settlement that October. The BHB's insistence that any deal had to be based on turnover was going to make negotiations extremely difficult and everyone was talking up the benefit that would accrue to bookmakers from GPT, and what it meant for racing. The BHB was seeking £150million for both data and pictures, compared with the current £80million. We offered a total of £110million, a figure that turned out to be virtually the same as the levy determination and picture deal produced.

Robert Hughes, the chairman of the Levy Board, had made it clear that he didn't want to be involved in the negotiations. He wanted the parties to agree between themselves and saw himself as the mediator. It didn't stop him describing our offer as "derisory" and indicating that he thought a good settlement would be around £130million. I don't know where that figure came from, except that it was halfway between what the BHB was seeking and what we were offering. As soon as Hughes called the bookmakers' offer "derisory", I knew there was no hope of an agreement.

We wanted two things: a settlement based on gross profits and an end to the levy as soon as a commercial deal came into force. We could see no justification for having both a levy and a commercial system running simultaneously and had received legal advice that such an arrangement would constitute illegal state aid. It seemed to me that you could have either a levy or a commercial payment but not both.

At one of the final meetings, we offered to withdraw our complaint to the OFT if a settlement was reached. If they would agree not to push for a commercial deal until the levy system ended, we were willing to discuss the basis for a commercial deal. Peter Savill, backed by Keith Brown, the Racecourse Association's chairman, told us that they didn't want us to withdraw our complaint to the OFT, which suggested to me that they didn't appreciate the seriousness of the OFT situation.

When the levy was referred to Tessa Jowell, Secretary of State at the DCMS, for determination, Hughes and the other two independent members recommended that the levy be turnover-based even though they had previously said they could support a gross-profits-based levy. I thought their submission was poorly argued and demonstrated a complete lack of understanding of the issues but I wasn't surprised. I get accused of being a dinosaur but they were the ones who were stuck in the mud, living in the past.

Tessa Jowell ignored the submission from the Levy Board members the government itself had appointed and decided that payments should be based on 10 per cent of bookmakers' gross profits. She did not, however, accept our proposal that the levy should cease as soon as commercial payments started, which I and others thought was wrong. The Bookmakers' Committee decided to seek a judicial review of the decision to run the levy and commercial systems in tandem.

I went on holiday and, much to the delight of the *Daily Telegraph's* Richard Evans, sports minister Richard Caborn, during a speech at BOLA's annual general meeting, berated the bookmakers for their decision to issue a letter saying they intended to seek legal redress. Evans evidently considered it our worst own goal of all time and quoted leading but unidentified betting industry sources suggesting that I was the inspiration and driving force behind the move. All I can say is that, while I was in full agreement with the unanimous decision of the Bookmakers' Committee, which was supported by the chief executives of both Ladbrokes and Corals, I wasn't even at the relevant meeting. I certainly didn't dictate Ladbrokes' and Corals' policies. Either Richard had an axe to grind or others were trying to absolve themselves from responsibility for the decision.

Negotiations with the BHB over data and picture rights eventually resumed. The 2.5 per cent of turnover the BHB had demanded covered both data and pictures. The bookmakers thought there was a better chance of agreeing a data deal if it was kept separate from a picture deal and the BHB agreed to this. We later discovered that the RCA had told the BHB that they didn't want them to negotiate the sale of pictures on their behalf. Nigel Smith, the BHB's commercial director, had visited both Ladbrokes and Corals to test out various proposals but not William Hill. Nevertheless, the BHB were in the right frame of mind to do a deal and a deal seemed to be possible based on 10 per cent of bookmakers' gross profits for data. After a couple of days' discussion and negotiation between a bookmakers' team led by me and a BHB team led by Peter Savill, a deal was done that was very similar to Jowell's levy determination.

While we were tidying up the details, Peter insisted that Ladbrokes and Corals make retrospective payments of 1 per cent of their past internet turnover for the data, something Hills had already been forced to do as the result of court action. Alan Ross, Ladbrokes' managing director, refused. To me, there was absolutely no logic in that, and the sum of money involved was small.

Ross went in to see Savill and when he came out I asked, "What did he say?" Ross said, "He's very upset." Savill came out, said, "The deal's off," and walked into the lift. Alan ran to the lift and told him he'd pay. We'd been negotiating for weeks and Ross was willing to risk the whole thing for the sake of about 80 grand, which he would have had to pay in the end, anyway.

I have to say that I agreed with Savill's position. In all negotiations, you shouldn't take irrational positions. There has to be a basis of logic. If I'd been Savill, I'd have done exactly the same. I wouldn't have said, "Oh, all right, then, it's only £80,000." I'd have said, "No. It is logical and fair that you pay it." The negotiations were tough and difficult but my respect for Peter and his negotiating skills and intellect increased substantially.

Having done the data deal we then moved on to pictures, negotiating with the Racecourse Association. They said they wanted £42million. I said, "Right, this can be a very quick meeting. There's no way we can pay that. I'd just like to remind you that we've just done a data deal worth £95million to racing. Without pictures, it would only produce about £75million, so you are starting with a picture deal worth minus £20million." That was the end of the first meeting. We could live without pictures; could the racecourses live without the income?

I then started to develop the idea that we wouldn't offer a fixed amount for pictures but would pay only for the pictures we wanted to use; in other words, a truly commercial deal. If we didn't get the pictures, because of abandonments, for instance, then we wouldn't pay for them. If there were six meetings and betting shops were only showing pictures from three, we would only pay for the pictures from those three meetings.

The RCA warned us that, in that situation, no one would want to stage racing in January because of the risk of abandonment and the loss of picture income. My response was that racecourses should insure against abandonment or put part of the money they got from the sale of picture rights into a central fund to cover abandonments. Nor would we pay for pictures available on terrestrial television because BBC and Channel 4 pictures were free-to-air. "If every single race, every day, was on the BBC," I said, "would we be sitting here talking about us paying you for the pictures?"

It was a better idea than I realised because, as soon as we suggested payments per race, smaller racecourses, including those run by Arena Leisure and Northern Racing, got very interested. Under the existing arrangements, they didn't think they got a fair share of the income from the Racecourse Association's picture contract with SIS, and they didn't have a lot of races broadcast on terrestrial television, free-to-air. The racecourses were falling out among themselves. In the end we agreed to offer £4,000 for each race shown in betting shops.

CHAPTER TEN
PLAYING THE GAME

When I was young, I never thought about having a bathroom and I never thought about owning a racehorse. Then I did have a bathroom and started to think about owning a racehorse.

In the 1980s, William Hill used to hold Golden Spurs award lunches and at one of them I found myself sitting next to Richard Holder. He was a trainer I admired, a good trainer of handicap and staying hurdlers, including Mayotte. Richard was very adept at placing horses to get the best out of them and, as I was to find out later, a very nice man.

By then I was established in Hill's management team, my financial situation was improving and I told Richard that, when I had the money, I was going to start a small syndicate to buy a three-year-old to go hurdling and I'd definitely send it to him.

A year or two later, at the same event, I was on Richard's table again and he hadn't forgotten. "When are you going to buy that horse?" "Soon, soon." I was beginning to get itchy to buy one and I saw an advert in *The Sporting Life* for a horse called Wahiba, for ten grand. I looked up Wahiba's form. He was a maiden three-year-old who had only run three times that year, for Gavin Pritchard-Gordon. He'd finished second in a claiming race at Salisbury and fourth at Catterick, when he was odds-on favourite and his saddle had slipped, and I thought he might be the horse I was looking for to win a little hurdle race.

My plan for buying horses in training is the same now as it was then, although Wahiba didn't fit the pattern completely. Every year, the big yards have a big clear out of horses. They don't have any choice. Sir Michael Stoute, for instance, has got almost 200 horses in his yard and almost 70 of them are three-year-olds. At the end of the year, he's got to find room for about 90 yearlings. So he's a forced seller and because he's got to sell so many, they're not all bad.

I always look for one who has been placed but prefer it to have won at least a little race, which Wahiba hadn't, but I was also a big fan of Ken Hussey's speed figures. Ken worked for *Raceform's* Handicap Book under the nom de plume of Split Second. Ratings based on time were commonplace in the USA but, at that time, were uncommon here. Ken was a pioneer in this country and, for me, the king of the speed figure compilers.

For a horse to qualify for my buying system, Ken had to have given it a rating of at least 40, out of 100. I think Wahiba had a rating of 41. I'd got a syndicate of seven together, so it wouldn't cost any of us too much, and asked Holder if he'd look at Wahiba next time he was in Newmarket. Three weeks later, he phoned me. He'd just been to Pritchard-Gordon's yard and the horse was still for sale.

"What do you think?" I asked.

"Well," said Richard, "put it this way. Head on, he looks like two planks of wood nailed together. It doesn't look as if he eats. He's skin and bone. They took him on to the gallops and he bolted for one and a half miles. He's completely nuts. The only good thing you can say about him is that he does run. They can't stop him running. If we can get him to calm down then, for the price, he might do the job and win a little novice hurdle for you."

Richard thought that walking Wahiba around the woods near his yard close to Bristol, in a quieter, less open environment than Newmarket, might calm the horse down. So we offered six grand and ended up paying seven and a half.

Then we had to decide on the colours. Bill Wilson, who later ran Raceline, suggested the Queen's colours, reversed. Bill said, "If they're good enough for the Queen, they're good enough for us." The Queen's colours were purple, gold braid, scarlet sleeves, black cap with gold fringe. Ours were red, purple sleeves with red armlets, black cap with a yellow star. They stood out a mile away. They were the colours I would eventually take over as my own and the ones that Shooting Light would eventually carry in his finest hour, when winning the Thomas Pink Gold Cup at Cheltenham.

Several years after modelling our racing colours on those of the Queen, I was lucky enough to meet her. In March 1994, I received a phone call from John Sanderson, Doncaster's manager, to say that the Queen was visiting the town on Friday 25 March and had expressed a wish to spend an hour at the racecourse. The hour coincided with one of our sponsored races, the William Hill Spring Mile. Would we allow her to present our trophy?

We sat on the balcony before the race, chatting, and, afterwards, the Queen presented the trophy to the winning owner of Glowing Jade. It's rather daunting to meet the Queen but she is very knowledgeable about racing and it was very enjoyable.

On a less exalted level, Wahiba had his first hurdle race at Huntingdon on 31 August 1987, the first horse to run in my name, albeit as part of a syndicate. There were 13 runners, most of them having their first run over hurdles but one, Daffodil, had already won three races and was odds-on favourite. Other than that, we thought Wahiba had a good chance and he was joint-second favourite. At the third hurdle, Daffodil fell. Wahiba was pulling Nigel Coleman's arms out but he was going well and made ground three out then, as they came into the straight, they came over to the stands side and out of view from where I was standing.

The commentator said, "Wahiba is moving up to join the leaders." A few seconds later, he'd fallen at the second last. A few seconds after that, we were relieved to see him career past the stand, riderless. A possible winning start had been lost but, to look on the bright side, he'd shown that he could win a race.

Ten days later, we ran him at Newton Abbot. He was the 2-1 second favourite and he finished a well-beaten seventh. It was very disappointing. I'd invited Richard to join us at a meeting at Ascot soon afterwards and he said to me, "John, I've got to talk to you. This horse is useless and still a nutcase. We'll have to run him in a seller. There's a nice little seller coming up at Hereford." I said, "Richard, I've waited 30 years to own a racehorse. We are not putting him in a seller."

Looking at the form book, I thought that Wahiba's best Flat form had been on the stiffer tracks, so I pushed Richard to run him at Cheltenham early in October. Richard wasn't very keen but that's what we did. A party of German bookmakers had come over, who I was supposed to entertain, so I took them with us. It was the last race, it was pouring with rain, the German party left before the race, the rest of us got soaking wet in the parade ring, there were 18 runners and Wahiba was 16-1.

You couldn't see the race through the mist and rain. I was standing with Bob Taylor, who was in the syndicate, both of us trying to pick Wahiba out in the failing light. As they came down the hill into the straight I spotted a horse with red colours right at the back. I turned to Bob and said, "He's last." Bob said, "No, he's fourth." I was looking at the wrong horse.

Wahiba rattled up the hill and finished second to Rivers Secret, who was winning for the fifth time that season. Our horse was beaten 12 lengths but I thought, this is more like it, especially when, ten days later, the horse that had finished third, Combermere, came out and won at Kempton. So off we went to Newbury, where we were up against one of Martin Pipe's: Sea Island.

In the paddock, Nigel Coleman, our jockey, said that Peter

Scudamore, Sea Island's rider, had told him that his mount, who was the favourite, couldn't jump very well. Up to a point, he was right. Sea Island charged off in front, stopped almost dead at the first hurdle, jumped straight up in the air, and charged off again. He did the same at the next hurdle, jumped left at the third, but then got the hang of it and jumped fluently. Wahiba had given Sea Island a long lead and couldn't catch him but it seemed to me that Nigel might have given him too much to do and we were only beaten two lengths, with the third horse 20 lengths back.

We were getting closer and our day finally came at Sandown on 4 December 1987, at 16-1, which reflected the fact that the company was stronger. Royal Illusion had won his only two hurdle races and finished the season as one of the top novices, winning the Victor Ludorum at Haydock and the Glenlivet Anniversary Hurdle at Liverpool. South Parade, the favourite, had actually been beaten by Daffodil on his previous run but went on to win the Summit Hurdle at Lingfield and Finale Hurdle at Chepstow. For a moment, it looked as if we might be beaten again because as Wahiba came to challenge South Parade at the last he got hampered by a loose horse, but he got there. "Great", I thought. Triumph Hurdle, here we come.

Two months later, it wasn't looking so rosy. Wahiba was beaten 15 lengths by South Parade at Chepstow in December, then almost 20 lengths by Kribensis and various others at Doncaster in January. Richard said that, if we were serious about going to the Festival, we had to give Wahiba a break. So we did.

A few days before the Triumph Hurdle, Richard phoned to say that he had just taken Wahiba to Wincanton to do a serious piece of work with Star of a Gunner, who had won the Lincoln the previous year and was being prepared for another crack at it. Holder said, "Either Star of a Gunner has got no bloody chance in the Lincoln or Wahiba is going to go close in the Triumph. I told Nigel to sit behind Star of a Gunner and another miler and do his best when they pulled away at the end of the gallop but he not only stayed with them, he waltzed past them and beat them four lengths. He's never been better."

We were hoping it would stay dry because it had been soft when Wahiba had been well beaten at Chepstow and Doncaster but it didn't stay dry and, the day before the race, we thought about pulling him out. I'm glad we didn't. It was one of the most exciting days of my racing life.

Wahiba was 66-1; a no-hoper to most people. Coming down the hill, he was fourth. Nigel pulled his goggles down. When they got to the last, he was only half a length down on Kribensis. Kribensis was a class horse. On the Flat, with Michael Stoute, he'd been rated 103, literally twice as good as Wahiba. He was still with Stoute, and still owned by Sheikh Mohammed – their first runner over hurdles – and we were fighting it out with them for the Triumph Hurdle.

I still sometimes listen to Peter O'Sullevan's commentary. "It's Kribensis from Wahiba from Chatam. As they come to the last, these three have the Triumph Hurdle between them." Richard Holder was shouting his head off; we all were. I'd had £50 each-way at 66-1, which at that time was a big bet for me, but the thrill of winning at Cheltenham would have been far greater than winning the bet.

Kribensis was just too good. Wahiba was beaten three lengths but what a performance! I turned round to Bob Taylor and said, "If the ground had been good, we'd have beaten him." I hadn't noticed Michael Stoute standing close by. "Rubbish," said Stoute, or words to that effect. "On good ground, we'd have beaten you more easily." A small group within the syndicate had also backed Wahiba each-way on the Tote – he paid almost 50-1 for a place, and we'd done 25 £2 dual forecasts, Wahiba with the field. Even with Kribensis winning, the forecast paid £1228 for £1. What fun!

Kribensis went on to win the Champion Hurdle. I'd like to report that Wahiba did as well, but the Triumph turned out to be the peak of his career. Remarkably, the following year, Richard Holder and Nigel Coleman got their revenge when Ikdam won the Triumph Hurdle at 66-1, beating a horse owned by Sheikh Mohammed: Highland Bud. Racing certainly is a funny game.

That autumn, we took Wahiba to the USA. It wasn't a success and he was never the same again. He did win the Doug Barrott Hurdle at Sandown at the end of 1989, over two miles five furlongs, but shortly afterwards he ruptured a tendon so badly that he had to be put down. By then, I'd moved to Leeds, been made redundant, been taken on by George Walker, and was about to be William Hill's chief executive.

For a time, racehorse ownership had to take a back seat. Over the years, there were also long spells when I didn't bet, particularly in my early married life, when things were really difficult financially. To be successful at betting, it must not be undertaken under pressure, when money is tight, but it was something I'd always done and, since 1983, I've kept records of my betting. If you are going to win, you have got to keep a record, partly because there is nothing more painful or more likely to make you be careful than watching the losses rack up in front of your eyes.

I got to the stage where, over 10 years, I was 25 grand behind. I had served my apprenticeship and had learned the hard and painful way. Then, at Uttoxeter one year, I won close to 20 grand from the Tote, then won another 10 grand over the next few weeks, followed that with £30,000 profit at Glorious Goodwood and have never been behind since. At the moment, I'm £135,000 up. That's since 1983 and a lot of it was won when there were 9 per cent deductions. I suppose the financial return for every hour I've spent studying the form is pretty low but I just love the challenge.

The key to my betting profits, and my hero, was Ken Hussey. His speed figures had played a part in me buying Wahiba and, for me, he was the best; brilliant. I first started to use his figures in the 1960s and when they stopped appearing in *Raceform*'s Handicap Book the bottom fell out of my betting world.

Later, I discovered that Hussey was working for the *Racing & Football Outlook*. I wrote to him and, once again, he supplied me with figures. When I got set up on the computer, I'd feed them in and make a few adjustments of my own, for weight-for-age. I think it gave me an edge because it meant that I was looking at races in a different way from most people. Hussey's system threw up long-priced horses that often got in the frame and I'd always bet each-way, often in big handicaps. It was a sad day when Ken died in September 2003. I dread to think what it will do to my betting performance. He was the godfather of speed figures in the UK.

I'm quite proud of being a bookmaker who has shown that punters can win, although the reason I'm ahead is that I've had a couple of big wins. Two of them were at successive Goodwood Festival meetings and both were with Corals.

The evening before the opening day of Goodwood in 1998 I went through the races and decided what I wanted to back. The next morning I was going to see a barrister in Lincoln's Inn Fields. I walked along Holborn, bought a *Racing Post*, had a bacon sandwich and a cup of coffee, phoned Corals at 9.30am to put my bets on, then phoned Michael Blackburn.

I'd known Michael since the time he was chairman of Touche Ross and helped us with our claim against Grand Met in the early 1990s. He'd been a non-executive director of William Hill from 1992 until Nomura bought us. Like me, Michael loved racing and betting and liked me to tell him what I fancied.

I'd picked three horses and taken the early morning prices. I had £100 each-way on Seignorial at 25-1, £200 each-way on Land Of Dreams at 11-2, and £200 each-way on Supply And Demand at 7-1. Then I had the same horses in three £20 each-way doubles and a £40 each-way treble, and a £5 each-way yankee with a fourth horse. Michael had also put his own bet on the same three horses.

I went to my meeting with the QC and had then got involved in a meeting at William Hill, when the phone rang. It was Michael. "Did you see it?" I said, "No, I've been in meetings." He said, "We've made a great start. The first one's gone in. Just got up on the line." That was Seignorial, SP 16-1.

I watched the other two races on television. Land Of Dreams travelled well throughout and was never going to get beaten while Supply And Demand – first-time blinkers and Kieren Fallon – landed a real gamble. So did we. I won about £75,000 and Michael also won a fair bit. I didn't want to waste the money, so I bought a second-hand red Bentley with my winnings. A big thank you to the Tote and Corals, and the fulfilment of an ambition to own my own Bentley. The very same day the next year, it happened again. The evening before, I phoned Michael. "I've got one for tomorrow," I told him. "I really fancy this." It was one of Paul Cole's, Mowbray, and I'd picked another one out, Ormelie, in the first.

The next morning I was up at the crack of dawn, got the *Racing Post*, opened it up and there was Pricewise's headline, "Take the 25-1 Mowbray." That's not what you want to see. "Oh, bollocks," I thought, "that's the price gone." I got on to Corals as soon as they opened, managed to get 20-1 or 25-1 on Mowbray — I can't remember which — and 12-1 Ormelie, had £100 each-way on each of them, and a £100 each-way double. They took the bets so, five minutes later, I phoned back and had another £100 each-way double and they took that as well.

Ormelie won at 6-1 and Mowbray, who had been backed down to 10-1, took it up two furlongs out and got home by two lengths. I ended up winning another £70,000, again from Corals.

At one time I was about £170,000 ahead; now it's £135,000. Needless to say, I'm well up with Corals and the Tote and with Victor Chandler. I'm a bit up with a few small internet companies, a bit down with Blue Square, a lot down with Skybet and most down with Ladbrokes, which grieves me. I cannot back a winner with them to save my life. Punters will know the feeling.

For a while I changed my style of betting and bet win only. I convinced myself I'd do better but I didn't. The change coincided with a change in *Raceform*'s speed figures, from the style championed by Ken Hussey to a new method championed by Dave Bellingham, which didn't take account of the weight carried in the saddle. The theory, which came from the USA and their speed figure king, Andy Beyer, was that the weight carried didn't affect a horse's performance. It might work on flat American dirt tracks, where most races have a limited weight range, but it flies in the face of the whole handicapping system in the UK and the shape of races here. I was very disappointed when *Raceform* changed from Hussey's tried, trusted and successful system. This led to a losing run for me and when I have a losing run I get very frustrated and upset. I am sure that is what has made me a winner in the long run.

I liked and needed speed figures and was told by a friend of mine, Robert Aird, himself a keen advocate of speed figures, that Ken was still working. Once I had found him and started getting his figures once more, normal winning service was resumed. It gave me great pleasure to phone Ken from time to time and talk to him about his figures and it was a very sad day when the great man died. However, he passed his knowledge on to others, one of whom, Dave Edwards, produces figures for Topspeed in the *Weekender*. I would commend them to anyone and the *Weekender* is well worth buying for those figures alone. Recently, they started to adjust the figures for weight-for-age, something I always did with Ken Hussey's figures.

From my records I find I do much better with my each-way betting than my win betting and, if you ever see a bookmaker offer to pay on the fourth place when a non-runner means there are only 15 runners in a handicap, dive in. When that happens, the odds are hugely in the punters' favour.

I enjoy reading books about betting, written by professional punters; how they make it pay and their views on various approaches to betting. I always considered the Placepot and the Scoop6 to be bad value bets. I used to think that, with a deduction of 27 per cent, you'd got no chance but I changed my mind after reading an article by American speed guru Andy Beyer, who was a great believer in their own Pick 6. Beyer argued that, over the six races covered by these bets, punters effectively face a take-out of 4.5 per cent a race, as opposed to what, over here, is now 13.5 per cent from the Win pool on each race. That means they are good value, especially as the pools include a lot of 'mug' money. He might be right but they are just not my type of bet. I just can't deal with six races in one day. I prefer to concentrate on one or two good handicaps, likely to be run at a strong pace, which means that the speed figures are more likely to work.

I haven't had a really big win for a couple of years now, although I've hit the crossbar a couple of times, but I love studying the form and having my bets. It isn't my betting, though, which enabled me to own racehorses, then own more of them. It was because I was lucky at William Hill. Lucky to keep passing 'Go' and collecting a lot more than the £200 you get in the game of Monopoly.

*

Financially, things worked out very strangely but very well for me. Things went wrong, disastrously wrong, sometimes – I got made redundant, Brent Walker got into horrendous trouble and finally went into administration, the National Lottery savaged our business, plans for two flotations failed. Yet I ended up a millionaire late on in my career.

When I'd moved to Leeds, under pressure, in 1988, I had a £120,000 mortgage and about £5,000 savings. Then Sears sold William Hill to Grand Met and I was made redundant. It was very worrying but Sears gave senior management a £50,000 bonus and Grand Met honoured our three-year rolling contracts, which gave me another £100,000 after tax and that enabled me to nearly clear my mortgage.

I'd hardly started work on the Raceline project, with Bob Lambert, when George Walker suddenly popped up from nowhere and paid me £600 a day. Within a year of being made redundant, I was back at William Hill, in charge, and at double the salary I had been on before.

In 1992, I got a £75,000 bonus related to work on Brent Walker's refinancing, although in my case it had more to do with my efforts in keeping William Hill going. On top of that, we'd struck a deal with George over Raceline that gave us a percentage of their profits above a certain sum, in compensation for Bob and I having had to abandon our rival project. That produced £70,000 in the first year. Later, when Raceline was sold, Bob and I each got £500,000.

Then, in 1993, there was an attempt to float William Hill, which failed. At the time it was a big disappointment because although there was no bonus involved, we would have been freed from Brent Walker, with all its debts, and been a publicly quoted company. As things turned out, it was a huge stroke of good luck. The banks drew up annual and exit bonus schemes for us. The annual scheme must have cost them £3million because, at my insistence, the scheme extended right down to area manager level. When Nomura bought William Hill, the exit bonus scheme meant that the management team all passed 'Go' again, and collected several million pounds.

Before long, Nomura had a flotation in their sights. One of the obstacles was that Bob and I had three-year rolling contracts and the other directors had two-year contracts. Nomura didn't think the Stock Exchange would approve of that, so wanted us all to go down to one-year contracts. In recognition of all our efforts, they offered to pay us one or two years' salary to buy the contracts out. We all agreed. When the flotation failed and Nomura sold William Hill to Cinven and CVC, early in 1999, the management team all passed 'Go' again. Lucky John. Lucky team.

The best was yet to come but I could already afford to buy a few more racehorses. I already had.

*

In the early 1990s, I ran a syndicate with shares in various horses with Micky Hammond at Middleham. I was living in Leeds, so it was convenient. I'd admired Micky as a jockey. I thought he rode with skill and intelligence and would make a good trainer. He didn't have a huge number of horses, so he could give time to members of syndicates.

In 1992, our small syndicate bought Liability Order out of Ron Boss's yard for 8,200 guineas and Micky won a couple of hurdle races and a novice chase with him. Then I was part of the syndicate that owned Daring Past, who ran in colours chosen by John Petty. He won seven races for us between 1994 and 1997. He broke down and we gave him to a friend of my secretary as a hack. She has had him ever since.

Eventually it came to the point where I wanted to buy a horse on my own, so in 1996 I went to the two-year-old breeze-up sales at Doncaster and bought a colt by Law Society for 11,500 guineas that I named Good Judge. A great name but he turned out to be of moderate ability and later died of colic.

Michael Blackburn had suggested that we buy a horse between us. Newmarket's July Sales were coming up and I picked two or three horses, using my system, including Shooting Light. He was a three-year-old from Michael Jarvis's yard who had struggled to win a maiden race at Hamilton on soft ground when a short-priced favourite but had put up good speed figures in several of his races, including when a well-beaten third to Persian Punch at Salisbury.

David Minton and Anthony Bromley, bloodstock agents, both took a look at Shooting Light and said that his hind legs were quite wide apart at the hocks, which wasn't an attractive trait. Although he wasn't the best of walkers – in fact, to my eyes, when he walked he looked rather ungainly – both agents liked him. I wasn't sure and almost let him go. Having decided to wait for the October sales, I then changed my mind and talked myself and Michael into bidding for him. Anthony Bromley bought Shooting Light on our behalf for 21,000 guineas, with David Elsworth, the trainer of Persian Punch, the underbidder. Michael wanted him to be trained in the south. We vacillated between sending him to Martin Pipe or Pat and Louise Murphy. Richard Holder had died, Louise was his daughter, and she and Pat had taken over Richard's yard. We decided to send him to Pat and Louise.

We ran Shooting Light on the Flat three times, and each time he ran progressively worse, ending up by finishing 17th of 18 on the last leg of Frankie Dettori's 'Magnificent Seven' at Ascot on 28 September 1996. It was a historic day, but not in the way in which I had hoped. After Frankie had won the first three races, I phoned the office and spoke to Richard Banks, who wouldn't normally have been in charge that day but was. He had already decided to hedge on Dettori's fourth mount, Decorated Hero, who came in from 12-1 to 7-1. Richard's decision saved us a fortune.

After the fifth race, I spoke to him again. He had already shortened Fujiyama Crest, Frankie's ride in the last race, from 12-1 to 9-2 but was still laying it to the trade. I told him to cut it to 5-2, to kill it. We and every other off-course bookmaker were backing Fujiyama Crest. The course layers thought Christmas had come early. They were laying 9-4 and 2-1 against a 12-1 chance and we were all falling over each other to back it. Several of them, notably Gary Wiltshire, took us on and it became obvious that the price wasn't going to shorten any more, so we stopped backing it.

In the parade ring, I jokingly told Tim Sprake, who was riding Shooting Light, that if he got anywhere near Dettori, he should knock him off his horse. Shooting Light was soon well behind Fujiyama Crest and history was made. For bookmakers, it was the biggest battering in the history of bookmaking.

Instead of the hoped-for celebratory meal, I spent that Saturday evening working out how we were going to arrange for £8million to be ready and waiting on Monday morning, in cash, to pay out winning customers. There were an awful lot of them and it would look bad, especially as we were part of Brent Walker, if we ran out of bank notes.

I had all our team in on the Sunday morning and got our banks out of bed as well. Not everyone, we hoped, would want to be paid in cash but, if they did, we had to be ready. No company sits with £8million in its current account, just in case it's needed, but we managed to have the cash ready. Shooting Light's run had been disappointing, as well as the £8million loss, so it was a relief when he won his first race over hurdles, at Sandown that November, and won it well.

We then went to Newbury, where Shooting Light lost ground at the start and was beaten five lengths by White Sea, who later started favourite for the Triumph Hurdle. It was good form. Shooting Light then won the Grade 2 Finesse Hurdle at Cheltenham and we were all set to go to Cheltenham with a real chance – better than we'd seemed to have with Wahiba nine years earlier.

Richard Dunwoody had ridden Shooting Light at Cheltenham and, afterwards, I asked if he'd ride him at the Festival. Richard wouldn't commit himself straight away but did ride and Shooting Light ran really well to be third to Commanche Court and Circus Star, beaten just over two lengths.

We didn't run him over hurdles again that season and his next race was on the Flat, at Sandown at the end of August, when Shooting Light won a staying handicap at 14-1. The prize money was poor – £3,225 – but I was thrilled. It was my first Flat winner.

Just over a month later, I had another, at Lingfield, with Iris May, a two-year-old filly I owned in partnership with Megan Dennis, trained by Jack Berry. Megan is the wife of bookmaker Gordon Dennis. Iris May was one of three two-year-olds I'd bought at the previous autumn's yearling sales, with breeding in mind.

I'd always been an admirer of Sir Mark Prescott's record as a trainer and thought that, if I ever had Flat horses in training, I would like to send one to him. At the 1996 October sales, I bumped into him. I was standing watching a yearling walk around the pre-sales ring when I turned round and saw Sir Mark next to me.

"Oh, Sir Mark, could I have a word with you?" I asked. "I really admire you as a trainer. I've always wanted to have a horse with you. I'm thinking of buying one of those in the ring now. I don't suppose you've got room for more horses or owners?"

He asked which horse I was interested in and then asked how much I was thinking of bidding for it. "15 grand." He said, "If you can get that for 15 grand, you'll have got yourself a very nice horse. And you are right in your supposition that I don't have room for any more horses or owners." Then he said, "But I suppose I've always got room for a nice fellow." That was me out. "That's a pity," I said.

Prescott turned away, then turned back and said, "Anyway, who the bloody hell are you?" "My name's John Brown. I run William

Hill." We arranged that I'd ring him at 7.00pm that evening. The horse I'd wanted went for 100,000 guineas. I didn't buy it.

I rang Mark and told him that I was chief executive of Hills but that I never asked my trainers about any horses in the yard other than my own. The only exception was that if there was a race coming up with an ante-post market and one of his was in the betting, I might ask whether or not it was going to run, because we didn't like having non-runners on our lists.

Prescott said, "Since you've been so frank with me, I'll tell you the Heath House rules. If I take a horse of yours, the vet's bills are going to be very expensive and there are no circumstances under which you are allowed to query them. You can query anything else but not the vet's bill. Unhealthy horses don't win races and the bills are going to be expensive because your horse will be vetted every week. "I will phone you every Sunday morning. I don't suppose I shall miss two Sundays in any one year and when I phone I will tell you how the horse has been for the last week, how he is today and what we are going to do with him over the next week. So there are no circumstances under which you need to phone me, unless there is an absolute emergency. I can't run a stable if I'm forever talking to owners, so I phone them all on Sunday morning. It takes me five hours and I don't expect to hear from them again.

"George Duffield rides. We don't debate who is going to ride the horse: George Duffield rides the horse. If he doesn't ride it, Seb Sanders rides it. If he doesn't ride it, C. Nutter does."

"Who's C. Nutter?" I asked. He replied, "You needn't worry. He only rides one or two a year."

"How much do you charge to train?" He said, "I don't know. You'll have to ask my secretary but it's expensive."

"Well," I said. "Will you take one or not?"

"Yes, all right then."

So one of the yearlings I bought at the October sales went to Heath House. She was called Liberte Bell, cost 15,500 guineas and, in late December, Mark phoned me and said, "I think she's probably useless. I don't think she's going to be a racehorse. I've been wrong in the past and they've surprised me but I'm not wrong very often." I thought, "Blimey, that didn't take very long."

Later on, Mark told me, "In my view, she's a filly who doesn't want to be a racehorse. We will have to sell her at the end of the year. I'm sure she'll dislike the fibresand so the only way we'll ever win a race with her is to run her on the all-weather, get a handicap mark, and she might just win a little race on the turf if we are extremely lucky."

So eventually, in May 1997, she appeared at Southwell. She did dislike the fibresand, stuck her head in the air, and finished second to last, beaten 25 lengths. She ran again at Southwell, then at Hamilton, well beaten, and then had three months off.

Sir Mark rang at the beginning of October and said, "We're running out of time. I've put her in the sales and you've got to sell her; she's no good. Her only chance is six furlongs on soft ground. I've got her in a nursery at Ayr." So she appeared at Ayr, running off a light weight, ridden by an apprentice, because John Lowe, who Prescott had intended should ride, was suspended and there wasn't anyone else suitable who could do the weight.

"I've told him how to ride her," said Prescott the evening before the race. "I've also written the instructions out for him. I'm going to ring him in the morning to make sure he's got the message but remember, Liberte Bell doesn't really want to be a racehorse and I think we will be lucky to finish in the frame."

So we knew where we stood; probably not in the winner's circle. She finished third, only beaten just over a length and we got seven grand for her at the sales. It was probably as much as she was worth.

The other yearling I'd bought was Foxie Lady. I sent her to Ed Dunlop and she managed to finish second three times as a three-year-old before deciding she didn't want to be a racehorse either. At the 1997 autumn sales, Michael Blackburn and I bought Shadiann from Luca Cumani's yard for 32,000 guineas and sent him to Pat Murphy's, where by then I also had a share in another syndicate horse, Another Night. Another Night won a race at

Chepstow for us the following spring while Shadiann eventually won four hurdle races.

But our main hopes centred on Shooting Light. He'd had such a good first season over jumps but his next three seasons were frustrating. He restarted promisingly, just getting beaten by Marello in the Tote Silver Trophy at Chepstow in November 1997 but although he put up some decent performances, including finishing seventh in the 1998 Champion Hurdle and seventh in that year's Cesarewitch, he didn't win.

Shooting Light missed the second half of the 1998/99 season with an injury and at the start of the following season we put him over fences. In his first chase at Exeter he finished third, which was disappointing given his hurdles form but Lord Noelie was a place in front of him and he went on to win the Royal & SunAlliance Chase at the Cheltenham Festival. Shooting Light then started even money favourite at Warwick but was soon behind. We'd been running him in a visor over hurdles and I thought he should be wearing it or blinkers over fences. Pat Murphy had thought he wouldn't need them over fences.

He wore them for his next run, back at Exeter, and was going well until he was brought down. A few days later, in November 1999, I was reading the *Racing Post* on the way to work and noticed that the Fighting Fifth Hurdle at Newcastle had been reopened because of insufficient entries. I got straight on the phone to Pat, who was about to phone me, and we decided to enter Shooting Light.

On the day of the race, there were nine runners but only three with any chance – Dato Star, who was odds-on, Crazy Horse and ours. It looked like prize money for nothing. Crazy Horse lived up to his name and ducked out at the second last and although Dato Star beat us easily enough, we won more than £8,000 for finishing second. Two weeks later, we picked up another £4,000 for finishing third in the Bula Hurdle at Cheltenham.

At the start of his next season, in November 2000, Shooting Light finished third in a novice chase at Exeter. It turned out to be no ordinary novice chase. The two in front of Shooting Light were Best Mate, soon to be a triple Cheltenham Gold Cup winner, and Bindaree, who went on to win the 2002 Grand National and 2003 Welsh National.

Shooting Light's next run was at Ascot a month later. Leighton Aspell had been riding Shooting Light and Pat liked to use Aspell, as he regularly rode out for him. There is nothing wrong with him; he is a good jump jockey who later won the Welsh National for Pat on Supreme Glory but Tony McCoy was available and, if you have the choice between anyone else and McCoy, it isn't a difficult choice. So we plumped for McCoy. We told him that Shooting Light wasn't the greatest jumper of fences in the world but that he got over them okay.

Three fences out, Star Of Dungannon, hard on the bridle, came to challenge Shooting Light, hard ridden, and looked certain to win but McCoy, at his strongest, forced Shooting Light to stay in contention and finally forced him back into the lead at the last and drove him clear. It was a great piece of riding. I don't think anyone else would have won on him that day. I don't think anyone else would even have kept the horse in the race. It was the first time Shooting Light had actually won over jumps since January 1997, almost four years earlier.

Pat and Louise had been having a lean time, desperate for a winner and, as Shooting Light walked in, led by Louise, she turned to McCoy and said, "Thank you, we really needed that." McCoy replied, "You didn't need it as much as me," even though he'd already ridden two winners that afternoon. That sums him up. Shooting Light had won but you couldn't say he'd been impressive and in his next race, without McCoy, he was well beaten, and was below form for the rest of the season.

That summer, 2001, Pat and Louise's marriage broke down and they decided to split up. We had to decide what to do with Shooting Light. Louise was thinking of setting up as a trainer and asked if we would let her keep him. We said yes but, on reflection, Louise decided that without the certainty of sufficient horses it would all be too much for her. However, she did prepare Shooting Light for the season to come.

Michael and I thought the horse would benefit from a complete change of surroundings and training regime, so we decided to send him to Martin Pipe. The horse was now a nine-year-old. On his arrival at Nicholashayne, Martin phoned and said he thought Shooting Light was a lovely big horse and, tongue in cheek, said we should have sent him there from the start.

Louise had said that the horse was about four weeks away from being ready to run but Martin said he wanted to take a little longer. After a month I asked Martin, "When's he going to run?" He replied, "Oh, not long. I want to make sure he wins first time out for you." I thought, "It'll probably be an ordinary little handicap" but when he did run him, it was in a very competitive handicap chase at Cheltenham, on the last day of October. I'd been preoccupied with negotiations about the levy and didn't have any chance to speak to Martin but I thought, "Christ, what's he doing?

We had another levy meeting on the day of the race so I couldn't go to Cheltenham. In the afternoon, during a break in the negotiations, I slipped out to a betting shop to watch it, had £400 on at 7-2, having missed 6-1, and he hacked up. The way he'd been running before, he had no right to win like that. He wasn't too clever at the first few fences but McCoy got him into a rhythm, travelling well and jumping well and he won on the bridle. It was amazing to watch because we were used to watching him struggling to go the pace and there he was, on the bridle.

When I got Martin on the phone, I said to him, "What have you done?" He replied, "He's fit now, John." I'm not saying that Shooting Light wasn't fit when he was with Pat Murphy but the change of environment and regime clearly suited him and Pipe has shown that he is a master at getting horses really fit. He has changed the face of training, changed his own profession and industry, and not many people can claim to have done that.

Trainers used to buy milers to go hurdling because they ambled round for a mile and a half and then raced over the last two hurdles. Now you've got to buy a horse that stays one and a half miles on the

Flat because they go so much faster. That's largely due to Martin Pipe. His horses would set off in front and go a decent pace because he knew that they were the fittest and, if they were the fittest, and he ran them like that, they'd win, and they did. He's one of the finest trainers I've ever known. Even now that everyone's woken up to his methods and tried to copy them, he's still managed to stay on top.

When Shooting Light won at Cheltenham, he was rated 123. As a hurdler, at his peak under Pat Murphy, he'd been rated 155, but that had been two years earlier. The handicapper put him up a full stone, to 137, for the Thomas Pink Gold Cup, at the same course on 17 November. It's always a very competitive race, it was worth £58,000 to the winner, and Martin said he thought we'd got every chance of winning, despite the 14lb rise.

I was in Florida and listened to the commentary on the telephone. As they approached the final fence, with Shooting Light in the lead, the commentator said, "The only thing that can beat Shooting Light is the last fence." I heard a tremendous roar of approval from the crowd and knew he'd landed on his feet because it wasn't the gasp or moan that you'd get if the 9-4 favourite, which is what he was, had come down.

I asked them to send a video of the race out to Florida and when I watched it, I couldn't believe that McCoy had managed to stay in the saddle after the terrible mistake the horse made at the fifth fence. It was a terrific performance. The handicapper then put Shooting Light up another 12lb, to 149 and we went to Ascot for the Tote Silver Cup Chase, over three miles. Punters have such confidence in Pipe and McCoy that, despite the hike in his rating, he was still sent off favourite, at 5-2. This time he won even more easily, by 11 lengths, and his handicap mark shot up again, to 162.

We decided to go for the Cheltenham Gold Cup without another race. That was probably a mistake. With hindsight, since he was in such good form, we should probably have gone for the Pillar Chase at the end of January. Shooting Light started joint-fourth favourite for the Gold Cup but he was never going, McCoy pulled him up and, later, he was found to have pulled a muscle in his back.

He ran really well on his comeback at Cheltenham in November 2002, giving away 20lb and more to the rest of the field but it was a three and a half-mile race and he didn't quite stay. It looked as if he was going to have another good season, although he'd be difficult to place, but he was then pulled up in the King George at Kempton, there was heat in his leg afterwards, and he missed the rest of the season with a tendon injury.

We sent Shooting Light back to Louise to look after then, after he'd had his leg fired, he returned to Martin for one more season. It turned out to be an amazing, memorable comeback. When Shooting Light finally reappeared, on Tote Gold Trophy day at Newbury on 14 February 2004, he was an 11-year-old and hadn't run for over 400 days. Not only that but, in the Grade 2, £40,000 Aon Chase, he was taking on Keen Leader, strongly fancied for the Cheltenham Gold Cup. To drive the point home, Tony McCoy had chosen to ride one of Martin's other runners, Seebald, so Richard Johnson was on ours. Not a bad substitute.

As Shooting Light was being saddled up, Martin told us that he knew the horse was in form, and the jockey was in form but, unfortunately, Martin wasn't. "Luckily, you're not the one who's got to run three miles and jump all those fences," I said.

It was the most exciting race I've ever experienced; even more exciting than when Shooting Light won the Thomas Pink Gold Cup – so emotional. We were hopeful that he'd run well but to see him go clear in the straight was a feeling I can't describe. We were waiting for him to blow up but, although he idled on the run-in, he didn't. Richard gave him a peach of a ride.

Shooting Light was fit and well, so we decided to run him in the Racing Post Chase at Kempton, where he was quite well in at the weights. Approaching the second last fence, he was just behind the leaders, although not going to win, when Tony McCoy felt something go. Shooting Light's hind leg had broken. Tony pulled him up as quickly as he could but there was nothing that could be done to save him, and he was put down. It was terribly sad and upsetting, especially as the plan had been to give him just one more race, in the Grand National, then retire him. Louise had already asked if she could have Shooting Light when he retired and neither Michael nor I could think of anywhere he would be more at home, or looked after better. She was very upset.

Shooting Light was a lovely character. You'd walk up to him and he'd stick his tongue out and want you to tickle it. He was a wonderful horse to have. He provided me with the highlights of my life as a racehorse owner, so far – him and Total Love.

I bought Total Love with Gordon Dennis at the 1998 sales. She was one of the few horses I have chosen that have leapt out as soon as I saw her. She was by Cadeaux Genereux, at that time my favourite sire. I thought she was lovely. We paid 52,000 guineas for her and sent her to Ed Dunlop.

From the moment he got her, Ed thought she was nice. She had her first race at York, where she was second, and then won a maiden race at Leicester, over six furlongs. A furlong out, it looked as if she would win easily but there was nothing between her cruising on the bridle and off it. She held on by three quarters of a length. We didn't know it at the time but that was to become a bit of a hallmark of hers. Gordon had always wanted to have a runner at Royal Ascot, so we ran her in the Queen Mary Stakes, but she ran disappointingly and was disappointing again on her next three runs. By then it was mid-September and Ed advised us to sell her. "What do you think we'd get for her?" I asked. He said, "Ten grand."

When I'd talked about her to Sir Mark Prescott he'd kindly passed on his experience that horses like her, that you thought were sprinters because of the speed they showed, sometimes stayed further than you thought they would. If you held them up as long as possible, it sometimes worked. They looked like sprinters but were suited by a mile, held up.

So I discussed it with Ed and we decided to try it, put her in a valuable seven-furlong nursery at Newmarket, and booked Michael

Kinane. Total Love carried top weight of 9st 7lb in the 19-runner field. Mick's instructions were to drop her out and see what happened. He dropped her right out, last in fact, and she stayed on really well and was beaten only a head, at 25-1. We felt fantastic. Sir Mark's advice had proved to be right. We were back.

Ed was soon on the phone to say that an agent had rung with an offer of 60 grand, with a view to taking Total Love to the USA. He said we should sell her. My reaction was, "She's rated 90. If I asked you to buy me a two-year-filly rated 90 for 60 grand, you couldn't do it. We're definitely not selling her."

Instead, we ran Total Love in a listed race at Ascot, this time over a mile. Dropped out again, this time by Richard Quinn, she was on the bridle turning for home, then got chopped off and the front two, French Fellow and One Step At A Time, got away. However, once in the clear, but five lengths down with only just over a furlong to go, Total Love flew and was only beaten a neck and half a length. In a few more strides, she might have won but at least she had been placed in a listed race. Robin, Ed's travelling head lad, said, "I suppose that's it for the season. She's run enough and is listed placed now." I told him, "Not likely. I am going to tell Ed to put her in the Rockfel next Saturday." Robin replied, "Shall I wash her down or take her straight there?"

We then got another tentative offer, this time for £200,000. I phoned Gordon and his view was that this was the first time we'd had a decent horse and he didn't want to sell her. So off we went to the Group 2 Rockfel Stakes over seven furlongs at Newmarket, the race after the Champion Stakes. Total Love ran really well but just wasn't quite good enough. She was beaten two necks by Lahan and Clog Dance.

Now that really was it for the season. Then we started talking about the 1000 Guineas. In the spring of 2000, we ran her in the Fred Darling Stakes at Newbury, in a gluepot. It was the first time I had ever flown to a race meeting and she ran terribly, with Lahan fourth. We gave the Guineas a miss but I still fancied Lahan and had £400 each-way on her at 25-1. She won, at 14-1, so the race still worked out well for me.

Total Love's season proved a frustrating one. In a race at Leicester, reminiscent of the one she'd won the previous year, she again looked certain to win but found nothing off the bridle and this time was beaten a short-head. In the Coronation Stakes at Royal Ascot, she finished a respectable fifth to Crimplene, staying on, and then six days later we succumbed to the temptation to take her to Newcastle for a small conditions race. It was a mistake. Total Love started odds on but finished only third and she never really recovered her best form.

At the end of the season, Ed Dunlop told us that he couldn't do any more with her and we sent her to Gerard Butler. He switched her back to sprints and she finished third in a listed race at Bath but became disappointing. So off she went to stud.

*

In 2001, another bookmaker, Fred Done, came up to me after a bookmakers' meeting and said he was thinking of buying a racehorse but didn't know how to go about it. Would I help? I gave him some advice, from my experience, and Fred joined the latest syndicate I had put together. Fred has built up the biggest independent bookmaking business in the country and gives his customers a lot of special offers and bonuses – he's known as the 'Bonus King'. He is the consummate marketing man, someone I like and respect: a real marketing man who makes things happen; it's not just guff and puff.

When we went to the 2001 Autumn Sales, Fred said that he'd like to buy a yearling for himself and his wife, Mo. Anthony Bromley had picked out a filly and a colt for us, both by Royal Applause, as possible purchases for the syndicate. I said to Fred, "Both look ideal, both are going to go for quite a bit, none of us are that clever, you pick the one you want and the syndicate will go for the other one." Fred thought about it, came back and said that he'd like to go for the colt, which his wife loved. "Thank God for that," said Robert Aird, who was in the syndicate with me. "I prefer the filly." I said, "So do I."

Mo Done did the bidding for the colt and bought him for 75,000 guineas. We had to go to 100,000 guineas, our maximum, for the filly. Both of them went to be trained by Mark Johnston. After the sales, we all went out for a meal and, over a bottle of champagne, Mo said, "I've decided what we're going to call our horse. He's going to be The Bonus King."

The following spring, we all went to Johnston's yard at Middleham to see how they were getting on. Mark brought out our filly, Sovereign Seal, and she looked magnificent, although Mark told us they were having a bit of trouble with her: she was turning out to be a bit of a moody cow.

Then he pulled out The Bonus King. He didn't look quite as good as I remembered him. He hadn't come in his coat, his head looked plain, and I thought, "How did we let Fred pay 75,000 guineas for that? I hope we haven't let him down." When we asked how he was going, Mark said he was a bit lazy and it was difficult to know how good he was. He was running him at Hamilton soon but he didn't really know how he'd go.

The Bonus King finished runner-up to Sir Albert, who later won a listed race at York. Within a fortnight, Fred's horse had won a maiden race at Ripon and then went to Epsom on Derby Day and won the listed Vodafone Woodcote Stakes and £23,200. Twelve days later, he was beaten a head at Royal Ascot, in the Group 3 Norfolk Stakes and, the following month, The Bonus King finished a close third in the Group 3 July Stakes. What a start with their first horse! Lucky Fred!

While The Bonus King was making hay, Sovereign Seal was eating it. The only thing she was bred to do was race, which was the one thing for which she showed absolutely no aptitude or desire to do. Mark Johnston told us that she was so bad that if a dozen horses were walking along the road a layman would look at them and pick her out as the worst because she'd walk along with her head down, full of lethargy.

She finally appeared on a racecourse, at Haydock at the end of September, but only to confirm our worst fears and, after three more fruitless efforts, we sold her for 6,000 guineas. Fortunately, Syndicate

2001 wasn't totally reliant on Sovereign Seal. We had more luck with another 100,000 guineas purchase, a Bering colt out of a Sadler's Wells mare that we named Tempsford. He didn't do much as a two-year-old but, in 2003, as a three-year-old, over longer distances, won five races, trained by Sir Mark Prescott. By the end of the season, he was rated 89 and we have kept him in training for 2004.

We also had Tourmalet with Alan Berry, who won as a two-year-old in 2002, and I was still involved with jumpers. That year, Michael Blackburn and I bought Fortune Island, who won a hurdle race at Exeter before finishing midfield in the Triumph Hurdle, which we still haven't won. Not so Lucky John, yet! The following month, April 2003, Fortune Island won the Queen's Prize on the Flat at Kempton for us before running disappointingly in the Chester Cup.

My racing interests have become quite extensive and I am now a racehorse breeder as well as an owner. At a *Timeform* Charity Dinner at York, I was introduced to Lennie Peacock, the widow of trainer Dick Peacock. I had happy memories of *Timeform*'s annual dinners, where I heard Lord Runcie, the former Archbishop of Canterbury, deliver one of the best speeches I have ever heard at a racing function.

Speaking in a wonderfully laid-back way, Lord Runcie recalled that his father had liked a bet and, consequently, what a disappointment his appointment as Archbishop of Canterbury had been to him. The next day, which was *Timeform* Charity Day, Runcie spotted a horse with an ecclesiastical name and told me he'd like to have a bet on it. How did he go about it? I told him he'd asked the right man. I opened a no limit Golden Spurs account for the former Archbishop of Canterbury but unfortunately there was no divine intervention and the horse lost.

A few years later, although seriously ill, Lord Runcie gave the blessing at the Saints and Sinners Christmas lunch at the Savoy Hotel. He blessed everyone there, especially the saints, then added, "For sinners, I can only advise you to repent or, if that doesn't appeal, back the favourite in the 2.30pm at Wetherby on Boxing Day." He was a very humorous man.

Lennie Peacock, a lovely lady, had bred Tirol, the winner of the 1990 English and Irish 2000 Guineas, and had a small stud farm at Middleham. She agreed to take Iris May, who had won twice for Megan Dennis and myself and finished third in the 1999 Gosforth Park Cup at Newcastle.

We sent Iris May to Cadeaux Genereux at Chris Harper's Whitsbury Manor Stud in Hampshire, which was particularly appropriate because Chris is William Hill's nephew. In March 2001, Iris May produced a colt we named Mr Independent and sent to Ed Dunlop. The following year, she produced a lovely strong colt by Mujadil called Joseph Henry and, in 2003, another by Royal Applause, while Total Love has had a filly foal by Mozart. Syndicate 2002 has three horses with Mark Johnston: Mister Monet, who won impressively at Sandown; Golden Quest, who has won twice on the sand; and Eternal Dancer, who has not shown much promise so far.

For my 60th birthday, in 2002, my wife Chris bought me a yearling she named Mr Moon. Moon is John McCririck's nickname for Chris (nee Shine). He is with Micky Hammond and I've also got a Kris colt with Gerard Butler called Pass Go. To think that it all started with an advert for Wahiba in *The Sporting Life*.

CHAPTER ELEVEN
PASSING GO

The introduction of gross profits tax gave the betting industry the tremendous boost I had predicted. We fulfilled our pledge to return our offshore business to the UK and introduce zero deductions for punters and business boomed. It was a turning point for the betting industry. Turnover shot up as customers reinvested their extra returns, telephone and, especially, internet betting took off, and the new tax regime made it viable to introduce low-percentage-deduction fixed-odds betting terminals in our shops. They were a roaring success.

In 2001, William Hill's profits from our shops, telephone betting and e-gaming were £118million; in 2002, the first full year after the switch to GPT, they were £150million: up 27 per cent. In 2003, they were just over £200million. We had absolutely pulled it off, in trumps. Bookmakers were better off, punters were better off, racing was better off and the government was better off, with the creation of thousands of jobs.

For Cinven and CVC, 2002 looked a good time for a flotation.

While I was negotiating with the BHB and the racecourses over the levy and data and picture rights, David Harding and Tom Singer concentrated on the flotation.

David had joined William Hill in August 2000 from the Prudential Group, having previously been responsible for the launch of Charles Schwab Europe's internet share trading business. He took over from me as chief executive that October, while Tom joined in January 2001 and, in March, took over as finance director from Bob Lambert, who retired.

There was a feeling that I shouldn't be too heavily involved in the build-up to the flotation, partly because, with David's appointment, there was a new structure to the future management team. Also, it seemed that I had upset most of the financial institutions during the previous, aborted flotation. I can't think why.

Because of that, Schroder Salomon Smith Barney, who coordinated the share offer, advised Cinven and CVC that it would be better for the selling price if I stood down as chairman but they still wanted me to stay on with William Hill, either as deputy chairman or as a non-executive director, and to carry on dealing with political matters. How did I feel about that? I told them how I felt, in no uncertain terms, because it deeply upset and hurt me that the two venture capitalists had even given it a second thought.

"I'm either chairman for the float," I told them, "or I'll leave now. You can choose and you can put that in the prospectus. You'll be floating with a chief executive who has been here 20 months and a finance director who has been here 15 months." I remained as chairman.

It seemed to me that they were trying to do what they thought would appease the institutions rather than what was right for the business and profits. In the end the institutions didn't seem to care who was chairman. They had lost out on a £600million profit by not backing William Hill's management last time and clearly weren't going to make the same mistake again.

David and Tom did an excellent job of selling the business to them and, this time, we had a better growth story to tell. There was

GPT and the internet, both producing rapid expansion and both likely to produce more, plus strong growth from fixed-odds betting terminals.

Initially, the indicative share price was between 190p and 240p, giving a mid-range valuation of £1.42billion. By mid-June 2002, with trading in William Hill plc's shares due to start on 20 June, the reception of the share offer had been so good, despite a shaky stock market, that the indicative price had narrowed to 220p to 230p, and was finally fixed at 225p, valuing Hills at £1.46billion. When trading closed on 20 June, the price had already risen to 241p. In April 2004, when the shares were well over £5 and the company's market valuation £2.3billion, William Hill was promoted to the FTSE 100 index – the index for blue chip companies.

Just over three years earlier, the City's financial institutions hadn't been prepared to pay £840million for William Hill. Now they were happy to pay £1.46billion. So the institutions lost out on over £600million, to the benefit of Cinven and CVC.

It was probably just as well that they didn't send me on the roadshow again because if they had asked me about growth I'd have told them, "Well, you didn't listen to me last time and it cost you £600million. Do you want to listen this time?" Those soppy analysts and institutions cost their clients a share of that £600million, and they were the people Schroder wanted to appease.

I've long held the view that most analysts only end up as analysts because they can't get a proper job and that most of them lack real integrity. This has been amply demonstrated by the heavy fines imposed on some of them for their advice to clients during the dot-com boom. As in all walks of life, there are exceptions but probably not many. The proof is in the pudding. All those analysts who advised against William Hill in 1999 for £840million then made it a buy in 2002 for £1.4billion were paid a lot for their advice. They all seem to know how to run your business, are always ready with advice on what to bet on, or what deal to do on the internet to get profits up. The trouble is, most of them have probably never run a business in their lives and they have certainly never been responsible for the results.

There'd been an even more extreme case a year earlier, when analysts working for Deutsche Bank, seeking to raise about £85million to fund Arena Leisure's involvement in Attheraces, supported predictions that Attheraces would have 23 per cent of the UK's horserace betting market by 2010, which was laughable. They reckoned Arena's business would be worth 148p a share. So far, they've struggled to get to 48p a share.

I don't have much time for analysts or merchant bankers. Analysts shouldn't be allowed to work for companies who have got a vested interest in selling shares in the companies that are being analysed. Of the 'professionals' I've worked with, I've always found lawyers the most impressive.

Bob Lambert's retirement ended a business partnership that had lasted almost 20 years, since his arrival as finance director in 1983. When we'd been made redundant, in 1989, we had formed our own company, Lambert Brown Limited, and had been a team ever since. David Harding described us as like an old married couple. We knew what each other was thinking almost before we thought it. We had even negotiated a contract with Brent Walker that contained a clause stipulating that if they got rid of one of us they had to get rid of both of us. We were able to do that because we were such a strong team, at a time when anyone thinking of buying or floating William Hill would have needed to have the management team onside.

Yet we aren't at all similar and had numerous differences of opinion, which helped with the decision-making process. Bob liked to get into the detail and wanted to get every detail right. He would happily spend hours analysing a problem or project to ensure that everything had been considered and covered. This attribute proved invaluable when Brent Walker got into trouble and in our many contract dealings with the banks and when we set up our offshore telephone venture. It meant that we never fell foul of the law on anything.

Bob was good for me because I was full of ideas and wanted to steam on like a prospector in a gold rush, crash, bang, wallop, and would surely have ended up in trouble if Bob hadn't been there, behind the scenes, quietly making sure everything was legal, the cash was there and everything was watertight. I often tell people that Bob was the rock, the solid foundation on which the success of William Hill was built, and I meant it. Without him, we would have failed.

When Cinven and CVC bought William Hill, the management team all passed 'Go' again. From the time when Brent Walker first decided to incentivise the top management to increase the capital value of the business by introducing an exit bonus scheme, Bob and I decided to share the potential benefits with the other directors and with the general management team, down to area level.

The same applied when Nomura exited and when Cinven and CVC exited, with the management board benefiting from a share scheme and other managers from an exit bonus scheme. Shares in the business were spread more widely than is often the case in such situations, which reduced the amount Bob and I received but increased the payments to others. As a result, ten members of the management team ended up as millionaires rather than just one or two and about seventy others received substantial payments.

For me, it all happened quite late in life, all really stemming from the day in 1989 when George Walker phoned me up and asked me to manage the 119 shops he'd just bought from Grand Met.

I realise how lucky I've been but it wasn't just luck. The payments I and others received were all given freely by successive owners of William Hill, shareholders grateful for our contribution to the increase in the capital value of the business. And its value had increased enormously, from about £570million when Brent Walker bought William Hill in 1989 (the final purchase price of £685million less the reduction following our successful claim) to £1.4billion at the time of Hill's flotation. Since the dark days after the launch of the National Lottery, William Hill's value had increased by £1billion. In total, the management shared between 5 per cent and 10 per cent of the increase.

When people asked me what I was going to do with the money

from the flotation, I told them, "I don't want to waste it. I'm going to have a bet, buy a few yearlings and get married." On 6 August 2002, three years after I had first asked her, I married Christine. I have one daughter, Jane, who was born in 1972, and I now have a grandson, Thomas, aged three, a real joy, as I suppose everyone's grandchildren are.

Funnily enough, Jane's godfather, John Trissler, used to live in the same East End street as me, Chobham Road. His father ran a grocer's shop opposite our own shop and was gambling mad. John, who is a few years younger than me, also worked for William Hill for a while and later, after working for Michael Tabor, had his own small chain of betting shops, which he has just sold. So at least two kids from 'tin bath' Chobham Road have made it and become millionaires.

I was so lucky to find Chris – Christine Shine – who worked at William Hill for many years. Chris remembers me going to work at a betting shop in the Grand Parade in Crawley one Saturday when she was a Saturday-only cashier, some 30 years ago, although I only really got to know her more recently when she joined Brent Walker and later became manager of William Hill's racecourse and events operation team. I couldn't have been luckier to find someone so nice with whom to share the rest of my life.

*

When David Harding joined, in 2000, I made it clear that I would stand back. When he became chief executive that October, I stood down from that position and became chairman.

I had always intended to retire before I was 65, if I could afford to do so. I couldn't wait to pack it in. I was almost 60 when William Hill was finally floated. I'd had my allotted time leading the company. You are either running a business or you are not running it: you can't be half-running it. As chief executive, I'd had to live with several chairmen and, in one way or another, all of them were a bleeding nuisance. When David succeeded me as chief executive and I carried on as chairman, I determined that I wouldn't linger on and make both myself and him unhappy, which in my view is what happens in such cases. In any event, I wanted to enjoy quality time with Christine.

For obvious reasons, I wanted to lead the company into the flotation and stay for the first annual general meeting afterwards but then I wanted to go. David and I have never fallen out or disagreed. He does it his way and couldn't have done a better job in getting the float away or seizing the opportunities presented by GPT. We couldn't have made a better choice for chief executive, from outside the betting industry. Now he has the chance to make his own mark and take William Hill on to bigger and better things.

I stepped down as chairman on 31 December 2003 and Chris and I now intend to spend a good few months each year in Florida, where we have bought a house that backs on to an inland waterway that leads to the Gulf of Mexico. I have also bought a 26-foot motor boat and taken lessons. Years ago, I had a boat on the Thames for a while so I knew a bit about it. It's great fun. You can sail along the coast, out into the bay, or moor outside a restaurant. But I still love my racing and betting, and will follow it wherever I am.

One of the horses I own is called Pass Go. There couldn't be a better-named horse for me. I've played the game, gone round the board, and kept passing 'Go'. I've been a Lucky John and a happy one.

INDEX